Graded Exercises in English
New Edition

Robert J. Dixson

Longman

Library of Congress Cataloging-in-Publication Data

Dixson, Robert James.
    Graded exercises in English / Robert J. Dixson. --New ed.
      p. cm.
    ISBN 0-13-298903-4
      1. English language--Textbooks for foreign speakers. 2. English
    language--Problems, exercises, etc.   I. Title
    PE 1128.D514   1994
    428.2'4--dc20   94-4779
                                          CIP

Acquisitions Editor: *Nancy Baxer*
Director of Production and Manufacturing: *David Riccardi*
Electronic Production Coordinator: *Molly Pike Riccardi*
Editorial Production/Design Manager: *Dominick Mosco*
Editorial/Production Supervision and Interior Design: *Dit Mosco*
Cover Design Coordinator: *Merle Krumper*
Cover Design: *Laura Ierardi*
Production Coordinator: *Ray Keating*

© 1994 by Prentice-Hall, Inc.
A Pearson Education Company
Pearson Education, 10 Bank Street, White Plains, NY 10606

Printed in the United States of America
20 19 18 17 16 15 14 13 12

ISBN 0-13-298903-4

Contents

To Be
Present Tense

I am	we are
you are	you are
he is	
she is	} they are
it is	

Supply the correct form of the present tense of to be as in the example.

1. She _____ a good writer.
    *(She **is** a good writer)*
2. They _____ old friends.
3. I _____ a student.
4. John _____ absent from work today.
5. We _____ both students.
6. The weather today _____ good.
7. The sky _____ clear.
8. Henry and John _____ brothers.
9. She and I _____ cousins.
10. I _____ sick today.
11. She _____ a business person.
12. You _____ a lawyer.
13. Today _____ Wednesday.
14. She and John _____ both good writers.
15. The police officer on the corner _____ busy with the traffic.
16. You _____ old friends.

To Be
Negatives and Questions

Form the negative of to be *by placing* not *after the verb.*

> I am an employee.
> I am *not* an employee.

Form questions with to be *by placing the verb before the subject.*

> They are absent from work today.
> *Are* they absent from work today?
> Why *are* they absent from work today?

A. *Change the following sentences from affirmative to negative as in the example.*

1. She is in Europe now.
   *(She **is not** in Europe now.)*
2. You are angry.
3. He and she are cousins.
4. He is very serious.
5. Both sisters are tall.
6. She is a clever woman.
7. They are members of the country club.
8. He is a good tennis player.
9. Elaine is a pilot with American Airlines.
10. The sky is very cloudy today.
11. The office of the supervisor is on the first floor.
12. It is cold today.
13. She is in her office.
14. It is a good movie.
15. The stamps are in my desk.
16. He is a smart man.

B. *Change the sentences in Exercise A from statements to questions as in the example.*

1. She is in Europe now.
   *(**Is she** in Europe now?)*

Plural Nouns

Most nouns form their plurals by adding s.

door → doors	doctor → doctors
pen → pens	apple → apples

Nouns ending in s, z, ch, sh, and x form their plurals by adding es.

box → boxes	class → classes
crash → crashes	church → churches

Some nouns have irregular plurals.

man → men	foot → feet
child → children	woman → women
tooth → teeth	mouse → mice

A. *Give the plural forms of these nouns:*

friend	*friends*	dish	_____
salesman	_____	glass	_____
buzz	_____	player	_____
orange	_____	foot	_____

B. *Change the following sentences from singular to plural as in the example.*

1. The pencil is on the desk.
   *(The **pencils are** on the desk.)*
2. The glass is in the kitchen.
3. It is a new dish.
4. The bus is at the corner.
5. The child is in the garden.
6. The clock is on the wall.
7. The watch is new.
8. It is a good picture.
9. He is a young man.
10. She is a young woman.
11. The dish is broken.
12. The tax is high.

A/An

A *changes to* an *before any word beginning with a vowel sound.*

a book	a man	a woman	a hotel
an apple	an orange	an umbrella	an hour

Complete the following sentences with a *or* an.

1. It is _____ lovely day.
   *(It is **a** lovely day.)*
2. It is ___an___ old building.
3. He is ___an___ unusual man.
4. It is ___an___ exception to the rule.
5. It is ___a___ long trip, but it is ___an___ easy trip.
6. It is ___a___ large building.
7. He is ___a___ honest man.
8. She is___a___ happy child.
9. The car is ___an___ used car.
10. It is ___a___ tall tree.
11. It is ___an___ egg.
12. It is ___an___ apple.
13. It is ___an___ old bus.
14. It is ___an___ empty milk carton.
15. It is ___a___ hour till lunch.
16. It is ___a___ windy day
17. The gift is ___a___ new book.
18. It is ___an___ one-story building.

To Have

Present Tense

I have	we have
you have	you have
he has	
she has	} they have
it has	

Complete the following sentences with the correct form of to have.

1. You __have__ a new car.
   (*You **have** a new car.*)
2. She __has__ one sister and two brothers.
3. You and I __have__ many things in common.
4. John __has__ a new wristwatch.
5. We __have__ many friends in St. Louis.
6. Helen __has__ a headache.
7. Grace __has__ a date with George tonight.
8. They __have__ strong accents.
9. Both brothers __have__ red hair.
10. The dog __has__ a long tail.
11. The office __have__ three large windows.
12. I __have__ a charge account at the department store.
13. Both children __have__ bad colds.
14. Dr. Smith __has__ many patients.
15. Ms. Jacobson, the lawyer, __has__ many clients.
16. We __have__ a large lunchroom at work.
17. The employee __has__ a new computer.
18. The building __have__ two entrances.
19. I __have__ brown eyes.
20. You __have__ green eyes.

Simple Present Tense

The simple present tense describes an action which goes on every day or all the time.

I work	we work
you work	you work
he works	
she works	} they work
it works	

Give the correct form of the present tense for the verb in parentheses.

1. She (read) the newspaper every day.
    *(She **reads** the newspaper every day.)*
2. We (come) to work by bus.
3. I always (walk) to the office.
4. You and I (play) cards every afternoon.
5. I (eat) lunch in the cafeteria every day.
6. Helen (work) very hard.
7. I (like) to sit in the sun.
8. The dog (chase) the cat all around the house.
9. Mr. Smith (work) for Eastern Airlines.
10. Gene generally (sit) at this desk.
11. We always (play) tennis on Saturdays.
12. We always (cook) dinner at home.
13. They (eat) lunch together every day.
14. Many employees (ride) the bus to work.
15. They (take) a lot of trips together.
16. We always (travel) by car.
17. You (attend) church every Sunday.
18. He (speak) several foreign languages.

Simple Present Tense

Add s *to form the 3rd person singular of most verbs. Add* es *instead of* s *in the following cases:*

a)   *when the verb ends in* o

go → goes   do → does

b)   *when the verb ends in* s, sh, ch, x, *or* z

reach → reaches   wash → washes   fix → fixes

c)   *when the verb ends in* y *(here, the* y *is changed to* i *before adding* es *if the* y *is preceded by a consonant)*

study → studies   cry → cries   marry → marries

A. *Give the correct form of the present tense for the verb in parentheses.*

1. Pat (go) there twice a week.
    *(Pat **goes** there twice a week.)*
2. Herb (do) the work of two people.
3. I always (try) to arrive everywhere on time.
4. George always (try) to do the same thing.
5. The supervisor (wish) to speak with you.
6. Mr. Walker (teach) English and mathematics.
7. They (go) to the movies twice a week.
8. We (watch) television almost every night.
9. Mary (play) the piano very well.
10. He (study) in the same class as I.
11. The father (watch) the children in the park
12. The mother (kiss) both boys good-bye every morning.
13. I often (catch) cold.
14. Helen also (catch) cold very often
15. She (do) all the work.
16. She (carry) her papers in a briefcase.

Simple Present Tense

B. *Change the subject in each of the following sentences from* I *to* He. *Use the correct form of the verb.*

1. I like to read.
   (**He likes** to read.)
2. I work hard.
3. I'm a good employee.
4. I own a car.
5. I'm an American.
6. I enjoy each English class.
7. I want to learn French.
8. I have a new wristwatch.
9. I speak Spanish.
10. I wish to learn English.
11. I read a book every night
12. I pass Mr. Smith on the street every day.
13. I always go to work by bus.
14. I try to learn ten new words every day.
15. I do a lot of favors for Pauline.
16. I play the violin very well.
17. I have two brothers and two sisters.
18. I always sit at this desk.
19. I do my homework assignments in the evening.
20. I study English three times a week.

C. *Change the subject of each sentence in Exercise B to* They. *Use the correct form of the verb.*

1. I like to read.
   (**They like** to read.)

D. *Change the subject of each sentence in Exercise B to* She. *Use the correct form of the verb.*

1. I like to read.
   (**She likes** to read.)

Plural Nouns

Nouns that end in y form their plurals in one of two ways:

if a vowel precedes the y, add s

key → keys   toy → toys   tray → trays

if a consonant precedes the y, change the y to i and add es

city → cities   lady → ladies   country → countries

Most nouns that end in f or fe form their plurals by changing their endings to ves.

wife → wives   leaf → leaves   half → halves

Nouns that end in o and are preceded by a consonant form their plurals by adding es.

hero → heroes   potato → potatoes

Change the subjects of the following sentences from singular to plural. Make any necessary changes in the verb form.

1. The child plays in the park every morning.
   *(The **children play** in the park every morning.)*
2. The knife is next to the plate.
3. The dish is on the table.
4. I have a new pen.
5. The plane leaves from the airport.
6. The bus stops at the corner.
7. The box is empty.
8. The church is near here.
9. The office opens at nine o'clock.
10. The man knows the lessons well.
11. I enjoy the work.
12. He is not afraid of dogs.
13. The boy does the work well.
14. The woman is ill.
15. The glass is broken.
16. The watch runs well.
17. The clerk is very polite
18. The key is on the table.

Possessive Adjectives

my	our
your	your
his	
her	their
its	

I like *my* teacher.   We eat *our* dinner at six o'clock.
She washes *her* car.   They are in *their* classroom.

Complete the following sentences with the possessive adjective which refers to the subject of the sentence.

1. She knows _____ lesson well.
   *(She knows **her** lesson well.)*
2. I also know __*my*__ lesson well.
3. Gail likes _____ vegetables very much.
4. I do _____ crossword puzzles on the bus every day.
5. You always get good grades on _____ examinations.
6. Both girls prepare _____ vegetables well.
7. Mr. Bach drives to work in _____ car.
8. Mary and I do _____ homework together.
9. Grace writes a letter to _____ aunt every week.
10. The dog wags _____ tail when it sees _____ dinner dish.
11. The children take _____ toys to the park.
12. I write the new words in _____ notebook.
13. Each cat has _____ own dish for food and water.
14. Both boys ride _____ bicycles to work.
15. You and Henry spend a lot of time on _____ crossword puzzles.
16. We enjoy _____ movies.
17. She always does well on all _____ examinations.

There Is, There Are

We use there is *with singular nouns; we use* there are *with plural nouns.*

> *There is* a book on the table.　　*There are* books on the table.
> *There is* one man in the room.　*There are* several men in the room.

Complete the following sentences with There is *or* There are.

1. _____ no Australians in this class.
   (There are no Australians in this class.)
2. _____ someone at the door.
3. _____ a lot of students absent today.
4. _____ a mailbox on the corner.
5. _____ three lamps in the room.
6. _____ two large windows in the room.
7. _____ only one door.
8. _____ a lot of desks in our office.
9. _____ nobody in the room now.
10. _____ a letter on the table for you.
11. _____ several beautiful parks in this city.
12. _____ twelve months in a year.
13. _____ only one cloud in the sky.
14. _____ no one at home.
15. _____ dishes but no silverware on the table.
16. _____ no stores in this section of town.

There Is, There Are

Negatives and Questions

The negative forms of there is *and* there are *are formed by placing* not *after the verb. The contracted forms* isn't *and* aren't *are generally used.*

There is a pencil in my bag.	There *isn't* a pencil in my bag.
There is *not* a pencil in my bag.	
There are two employees absent today.	There *aren't* two employees absent today.
There are *not* two employees absent today.	

The question forms of there is *and* there are *are formed by placing the verb before* there.

There is a window in the room.
Is there a window in the room?

There are four windows in the room.
Are there four windows in the room?

A. Change the following sentences from affirmative to negative. Use the contracted form.

1. There is a flag at the top of the building.
   *(There **isn't** a flag at the top of the building.)*
2. There are two lamps in the room.
3. There is a pillow on each bed.
4. There are two police officers on each corner.
5. There is a big parade today.
6. There are several doctors in this area.
7. There are ten new words in this lesson.
8. There is a message for you on the hall table.
9. There are enough chairs for everyone.
10. There are plenty of good seats available.
11. There is a comfortable chair in each room.
12. There is a good restaurant near here.
13. There are telephones in every room.
14. There are four dogs in the street.

B. Change the sentences in Exercise A to questions.

1. There is a flag at the top of the building.
   *(**Is there** a flag at the top of the building?)*

Possessive Form of Nouns

When a noun does not end in s, form the singular and sometimes the plural possessive by adding an apostrophe s ('s).

the boy → the *boy's* hat	the girl → the *girl's* ball
the lady → the *lady's* purse	the children → the *children's* games

When a noun already ends in s, form the singular possessive by adding an apostrophe s ('s) and form the plural possessive by adding only an apostrophe (').

the boss → the *boss's* chair	the boys → the *boys'* hats
Charles → *Charles's* book	the ladies → the *ladies'* purses

Note that the possessive is used even when the noun modified is not expressed.

She went to *Jonathan's.* (Jonathan's home)

I have an appointment at the *doctor's.* (the doctor's office)

Insert the apostrophe in the correct places in the following sentences.

1. Mrs. Reagans car is outside.
   *(Mrs. **Reagan's** car is outside.)*
2. I do all my shopping at Macys Department Store.
3. She buys her clothes in Chicagos best shops.
4. The mens room is just down the hall.
5. They sell ladies dresses on this floor.
6. The childs toys are all broken.
7. They sell childrens toys in this store.
8. There is a lot of competition between Bobs two sisters.
9. He goes to the doctors office once a week.
10. Dr. Smiths secretary is Mexican.
11. Lincolns Birthday is February 12.
12. Henry and Sallys father is in Europe.
13. Mrs. Jacksons daughter is eight years old.
14. St. Peters in Rome and St. Pauls in London are both good examples of Baroque architecture.

This/That; These/Those

This *indicates that something is near us; that indicates that it is at a distance*

> *This* book is in my hand.
> *That* book is over there on the table.

The plural of *this* is these; *the plural of* that *is* those.

> *These* books are in my hand.
> *Those* books are over there on the table.

Change the following sentences from singular to plural.

1. This exercise is easy.
   (These exercises are easy.)
2. This room is too small for our furniture.
3. That pen on the floor is Sarah's.
4. This stack of compact discs belongs to William.
5. That boy on the other side of the street is George's brother.
6. That book is out of date.
7. That purse on the table is Elizabeth's.
8. This is my chair.
9. That is Henry's pen.
10. This message is for you.
11. That letter on the table is for Ms. Thaler.
12. This is my pen, not Sandy's.
13. That mountain in the distance forms part of the Rocky Mountains.
14. This car belongs to my father.
15. That office at the end of the hall is the administration office.
16. This chair is very comfortable.

Object Pronouns

I	me	we	us
you	you	you	you
he	him		
she	her	} they	them
it	it		

Object pronouns are used as direct objects, indirect objects, and objects of prepositions.

She knows *me* well.

We give *her* our homework every day.

They give it to *us*.

A.   *Choose the correct object pronoun form.*

1.   I often see (they, them) after work.
     *(I often see **them** after work.)*
2.   She lives near (we, us).
3.   We always go to lunch together with (she, her).
4.   He teaches (we, us) English.
5.   She sits near (I, me) during class.
6.   I know both of (they, them) well.
7.   I always speak to (he, him) in English.
8.   What is the matter with (he, him) today?
9.   He explains the lesson to (we, us) each morning.
10. There are some letters here for you and (I, me).
11. We want to divide the money between (we, us).
12. The Venezuelan lady knows (they, them) both well.
13. I know her sister and (she, her).
14. Mr. Johnson often helps Susan and (I, me).
15. He sends (she, her) a lot of presents.
16. She seldom speaks to (we, us) in Spanish.
17. He looks at (she, her) during the class.
18. She always helps (I, me) with my clients.
19. He always sits between Amy and (I, me).
20. He wants to talk with (they, them).

Object Pronouns

B. *Substitute the correct object pronoun for the word or words in italics.*

1. I see *Mr. Park* during coffee break every morning.
    *(I see **him** during coffee break every morning.)*
2. I sit near *Grace and Frances* during the lesson.   . them
3. All the boys like *Joy* very much.
4. I often see you *and your sister* at the supermarket.   Them
5. He always goes to the movies with *his parents.*   Them
6. I know *both boys* very well.   they
7. Frank always waits for *Al and me* after work.   us
8. He drives *Sue and Cal* to work every morning.
9. I sit next to *Carlos.*   Him
10. I also sit directly in front of *Marsha.*   Her
11. He writes a lot of letters to *his relatives.*
12. This book belongs to *William.*   Him
13. I know *the dentist* very well.
14. The doctor relies on *her assistant.*
15. I understand *Miss McGrady.*   Her
16. He always speaks to *his students* in English.
17. Everyone in our house plays cards except *my brother.*
18. He sends *his parents* money every week.
19. I talked to *Mr. and Mrs. Nelson* yesterday.
20. She saw *the women* after school.

Imperative Form

The imperative form expresses a command or request. The subject you *(singular or plural) is understood but not expressed.*

> Come back later.   (You) come back later.   Wait outside.

The negative of the imperative form uses don't.

> Don't come back later.   Don't wait outside.

Please, *used at the beginning or end of an imperative sentence, makes it more polite.*

> *Please* come back later.   Wait outside, *please.*

A. *Give the imperative form of the following sentences.*

1. (Sit) there.
    (Sit there.)
2. (Give) this to Sally.
3. (Open) the door.
4. (Close) the door.
5. (Wait) in the outer office.
6. (Call) him in the morning.
7. (Let) him talk with her.
8. (Let) them talk.
9. (Turn) off the light.
10. (Put) your feet on the chair.
11. (Drop) this in the mailbox.
12. (Leave) your books there.
13. (Let) Alexandra know about this.
14. (Help) Jason with his homework.
15. (Send) money.

B. *Give the negative imperative form of the sentences in Exercise A.*

> (Sit) there.   *(**Don't** sit there.)*

C. *Make the sentences in Exercise A more polite by adding* please *at the beginning or end.*

> (Sit) there.   *(**Please** sit there.   Sit there, **please.**)*

Simple Present Tense

Negatives

Form the negative of the simple present tense by putting do not *or* does not *before the verb. The contracted forms* don't *and* doesn't *are generally used.*

I do not know (I don't know)	we do not know (we don't know)
you do not know (you don't know)	you do not know (you don't know)
he does not know (he doesn't know)	
she does not know (she doesn't know)	they do not know (they don't know)
it does not know (it doesn't know)	

Note that after does not (doesn't), *the verb does not have the* s *of the 3rd person singular affirmative statement.*

Change the following sentences from affirmative to negative. Use both the full form and the contracted form.

1. I work on the tenth floor.
   *(I **do not** work on the tenth floor. I **don't** work on the tenth floor.)*
2. Ella likes to study English.
3. You speak English well.
4. The plane leaves at ten o'clock.
5. He knows everyone in the office.
6. I feel good.
7. He eats lunch in the cafeteria every day.
8. She always comes to work late.
9. They live in Chicago.
10. We need a fan in this room.
11. Janet and I cook together.
12. I understand everything he says.
13. She wants to visit San Francisco.
14. He begins his new job this week.
15. The child plays in the park every afternoon.
16. Gina and James make mistakes in spelling.
17. It rains in the summer.
18. You own a watch.

Simple Present Tense
Questions

Form questions in the simple present tense by placing do *or* does *before the subject.*

Do I study?	Do we study?
Do you study?	Do you study?
Does he study?	
Does she study?	Do they study?
Does it study?	

Change the following statements to questions as in the example.

1. Patricia goes to class twice a week.
   (Does Patricia go to class twice a week?)
2. They enjoy their cooking lessons.
3. That company buys a lot of merchandise from us.
4. It looks like rain.
5. He drives to Washington once a week.
6. The committee meets on the third floor.
7. He seems to be very busy.
8. This book belongs to her.
9. You like New York.
10. You speak French well.
11. He often goes out of town.
12. I take the Number 65 bus to my new job.
13. They sell newspapers there.
14. The store opens at nine o'clock.
15. It closes at five-thirty.
16. He eats a lot of vegetables.
17. She lives in Los Angeles.
18. He and I sing too softly.
19. Tony and his mother play chess every day.

Simple Present Tense
Questions

Form simple present tense questions by placing do or does before the subject. Include questions that begin with question words like where, why, when, how, and what.

> Valerie lives alone.
> *Does* Valerie live alone?   Why *does* Valerie live alone?

A. Supply do or does to complete these present tense questions.

1. Where _____ Sam live?
   *(Where **does** Sam live?)*
2. How often _____ you go to the movies?
3. What time _____ the plane leave?
4. What language besides English _____ your teacher speak?
5. What time _____ you get up every morning?
6. What time _____ the rest of your family get up?
7. When _____ they get up every morning?
8. How well _____ Edna speak French?
9. Where _____ you usually meet Lois after the lesson?
10. How much _____ it cost to fly from Havana to Madrid?
11. How often_____ it rain during the month of April in your country?
12. How much _____ you generally pay for a pair of shoes?
13. How long _____ your meeting last?
14. What time _____ your meeting begin and what time does it end?
15. Where _____ you live?
16. How _____ you feel today?
17. Where _____ Ed go every day after work?
18. Where _____ you eat lunch every day?
19. What _____ you generally do over the weekend?
20. Which movie star _____ you like best?
21. Why _____ Jane want to study Russian?
22. How often _____ you go for a walk in the park?

Simple Present Tense
Questions

B. *Change the following sentences to questions beginning with the question word in parentheses.*

1. They live in Boston. (Where)
   (Where do they live?)
2. The play begins at eight o'clock. (What time)
3. They get home at six o'clock every night. (When)
4. The travel agent speaks French poorly. (How well)
5. Those books cost $8.95. (How much)
6. They travel by car. (How)
7. He comes here once a week. (How often)
8. She feels good. (How)
9. Francine wants to learn English in order to get a better job. (Why)
10. They meet on the corner every morning. (Where)
11. We go to the movies twice a week. (How often)
12. The banker goes to the park after the play. (Where)
13. We learn ten new words every day. (How many)
14. They eat lunch in the cafeteria. (Where)
15. He drives a Ford. (What kind of car)
16. This plate belongs on the shelf. (Where)
17. The committee meets in Room 10. (In which room)
18. She teaches us cooking. (What)
19. It rains in the spring. (When)
20. He gets up at seven o'clock every morning. (What time)
21. She goes to bed at ten o'clock. (When)

To Be
Past Tense

I was	we were
you were	you were
he was	
she was	} they were
it was	

Supply the correct form of the past tense of to be *as in the example.*

1. Teresa _____ absent from work yesterday.
   *(Teresa **was** absent from work yesterday.)*
2. He _were_ in the same office as Wendy last year.
3. They _were_ good friends for many years.
4. The office door _____ open.
5. But both windows _____ closed.
6. Ned _____ not at work yesterday.
7. He and his sister _were_ sick.
8. You _____ busy all day yesterday.
9. We _____ tired after our long walk.
10. I _____ hungry after so much exercise.
11. There _____ a lot of members absent from the meeting yesterday.
12. Fred _____ present, but I _____ not.
13. The weather yesterday _____ very warm.
14. We _____ pleased to receive your memorandum.
15. You _____ not satisfied with my memorandum.
16. The exercises in the last lesson _____ easy.
17. We _____ not able to get in touch with Mr. Reese yesterday.
18. The wind last night _____ very strong.

To Be
Past Tense Negatives and Questions

Form the negative of the past tense of to be *by placing* not *after the verb. The contracted forms* wasn't *and* weren't *are generally used.*

I was not (I wasn't)	we were not (we weren't)
you were not (you weren't)	you were not (you weren't)
he was not (he wasn't)	
she was not (she wasn't)	they were not (they weren't)
it was not (it wasn't)	

Form questions in the past tense of to be *by placing the verb before the subject.*

They were here yesterday.	Were they here yesterday?

A. **Change the following sentences from affirmative to negative. Use both the full form and the contracted form.**

1. You were tired last night.
   *(You **were not** tired last night. You **weren't** tired last night.)*
2. These doors were closed.
3. The exercises were easy to do.
4. The man was a stranger to her.
5. It was a pleasant day.
6. The sea was very rough.
7. He was a tall man.
8. There were ten new words in the lesson.
9. Sarah was a good swimmer.
10. She was very intelligent.
11. They were both Americans.
12. She was a good tennis player.
13. You were a happy child.
14. He was always angry.
15. They were friendly enemies.
16. Bert was an old friend of the family

B. **Change the sentences in Exercise A to questions.**

1. You were tired last night.
   (Were you tired last night?)

Past Tense
Regular Verbs

Form the past tense of regular verbs by adding ed *to their simple form.*

I worked	we worked
you worked	you worked
he worked	
she worked	} they worked
it worked	

Note these spellings:

live → lived   study → studied

Supply the past tense form of the verbs in parentheses.

1. We (work) in our garden all day yesterday.
   *(We **worked** in our garden all day yesterday.)*
2. I (listen) to the stereo until twelve o'clock last night.
3. Meg and I (talk) on the telephone yesterday.
4. He always (want) to learn English.
5. They (live) in France for many years.
6. We (expect) to go to Europe in June.
7. The meeting (last) about two hours.
8. We (change) planes in Seattle.
9. We both (like) the movies last night very much.
10. I (wait) almost two hours for Gertrude.
11. They (paint) their house white.
12. She (arrive) late to the meeting.
13. We (watch) television until eleven o'clock last night.
14. She (study) in our class last semester.
15. I (mail) your letter on my way to work.
16. We both (learn) how to swim many years ago.
17. Perry (marry) Barbara eight months ago.

Past Tense
Irregular Verbs

Irregular verbs, like regular verbs, have the same form in all persons of the past tense:

I ate	we ate
you ate	you ate
he ate, she ate, it ate	they ate

Memorize and practice the past tense forms of these irregular verbs:

begin → began	feel → felt	hear → heard	sell → sold
cost → cost	give → gave	put → put	speak → spoke
drink → drank	go → went	read → read	tell → told
eat → ate	have → had	see → saw	write → wrote

Supply the past tense form of the verbs in parentheses.

1. Mr. and Mrs. Rockwell (come) to visit us last night.
   *(Mr. and Mrs. Rockwell **came** to visit us last night.)*
2. They (tell) us about their plans for their new home.
3. The weather was warm, so we (sit) on our front porch.
4. I (put) your coat in the closet.
5. The meeting last night (begin) at eight and ended at ten.
6. I stayed home last night and (write) several letters.
7. I (see) you on the street yesterday.
8. This book (cost) $5.50.
9. I (eat) my lunch in the cafeteria yesterday.
10. The man (drink) a little wine at the party last night.
11. I (give) Joe your message and also (tell) him my ideas on the subject.
12. Ms. Reese finally (sell) her house.
13. I (hear) the President speak on television last night.
14. My father (know) Mr. Evans well even before he (come) to live in this town.
15. Kim (feel) well yesterday, but today she feels sick again.
16. We (go) to the park yesterday and I (get) wet when it rained.
17. I (read) the novel several years ago.
18. You (have) a cold last week.
19. Senator Jordan (speak) to our club last month.

Past Tense
Negatives

Form past tense negatives by placing did not *before the verb and by changing the verb to its simple form. The contracted form* didn't *is generally used.*

I *went.*   I *did not* go.   I *didn't* go.

I did not see (I didn't see)	we did not see (we didn't see)
you did not see (you didn't see)	you did not see (you didn't see)
he did not see (he didn't see)	
she did not see (she didn't see)	they did not see
it did not see (it didn't see)	(they didn't see)

Change the following sentences from affirmative to negative. Use both the full form and the contracted form.

1. They ate chicken for dinner.
   *(They **did not eat** chicken for dinner.*
   *They **didn't eat** chicken for dinner)*
2. You told me about it.
3. He put the books on the table.
4. They stayed in Mexico City.
5. Judy and I saw Eliot yesterday.
6. He planned his work well.
7. The meeting lasted a long time.
8. The book cost $3.95.
9. The woman and her husband worked together.
10. I knew him very well.
11. They sold their home.
12. I spoke with George about that matter.
13. She came to the meeting alone.
14. We sat together at the concert last night.
15. I went to Bermuda by boat.
16. You gave her your message.

Past Tense
Questions

Form past tense questions by placing did *before the subject and by changing the verb to its simple form.*

She went home.	*Did* she go home?

did I work	did we work
did you work	did you work
did he work	
did she work	} did they work
did it work	

A. *Change the following past tense statements to questions as in the example.*

1. She lived in Peru for two years.
   (Did she live in Peru for two years?)
2. He gave her a lot of presents.
3. They stayed in Europe all summer.
4. She told them all about her trip.
5. You moved here in February.
6. Terry flew to Minneapolis.
7. We went home after you did last night.
8. They came to the party together.
9. Carla and Dave knew each other as children.
10. He worked in that firm for many years.
11. She felt much better after her operation.
12. The meeting began on time.
13. I passed all my examinations.
14. They put him in the advanced class.
15. I gave you my new telephone number.
16. The crowd waited a long time to see the President.

Past Tense
Questions

B. *Change the following past tense statements to questions beginning with the question word in parentheses.*

1. Marianne arrived at ten o'clock. (What time)
   (What time did Marianne arrive?)
2. They sold their home last week. (When)
3. The meeting began at eight-thirty. (What time)
4. The tickets cost three dollars. (How much)
5. He paid for the car by check. (How)
6. She invested ten thousand dollars in the stock market. (How much)
7. They sat in the first row. (In which row)
8. He spoke to them in French. (In what language)
9. The meeting lasted two hours. (How long)
10. It began at eight o'clock. (What time)
11. I telephoned her at two o'clock. (What time)
12. He went to Denver to see some friends. (Why)
13. You mentioned it to him three or four times. (How many times)
14. They ate lunch in the park. (Where)
15. We worked there for five years. (How many years)
16. I put the mail on Mr. Agee's desk. (Where)
17. She waited for them for an hour. (How long)
18. We got home around midnight. (What time)
19. He walked to the meeting with Peg. (Who)
20. You went to the park after the lesson. (Where)

Adjectives and Adverbs

Adjectives modify nouns.

> a *large* tree   an *open* door

Adverbs modify verbs. They tell how we do something.

> He speaks *slowly.*   They work *rapidly.*

We can form many adverbs by adding ly *to an adjective.*

> soft   softly
> careful   carefully
> easy (y to i) easily

We can use a few words like fast, hard, late, *and* low *as either adjectives or adverbs without any changes in form.*

> He is a *hard* worker.   He works *hard.*

Supply the appropriate form of the adjective or adverb.

1. She is a _____ (careful) student. She always does her homework _____ (careful).
   *(She is a **careful** student. She always does her homework **carefully**.)*
2. The baseball player hit the ball _____ (hard).
3. Come _____ (quick). We need your help.
4. You should drive _____ (slow) along this dangerous road.
5. The old man walks very _____ (slow).
6. Pam is a very _____ (slow) learner.
7. Her brother, on the other hand, learns _____ (rapid).
8. Mr. Gonzalez has a _____ (permanent) visa.
9. He hopes to remain in this country _____ (permanent).
10. This is an _____ (easy) exercise.
11. I can do all of these exercises _____ (easy).
12. Ada works very _____ (hard) in her new job.
13. You walk very _____ (fast).
14. We are both _____ (serious) employees.
15. We both study English very _____ (serious).
16. I agree with you_____ (complete) in that matter.
17. This apple is very _____ (soft).
18. She always speaks _____ (soft) to the child.
19. Pete is a _____ (beautiful) kitten.
20. My sister plays the violin _____ (beautiful).

Good, Well

Good *is an adjective and must modify a noun.*

> She is a *good* student.

Well *is usually used as an adverb.*

> She works *well.*

Well *is occasionally used as an adjective. It is used as an adjective only when it means* to be in good health.

> John was sick, but now he is *well.*

Supply good *or* well *in the following sentences.*

1. He does his work _____.
   *(He does his work **well.**)*
2. He plays the piano very _____.
3. He is a _____ pianist.
4. This pen does not work _____.
5. Our lunch today was very _____.
6. These exercises are _____ for us.
7. I was sick for a few days, but now I am _____ again.
8. How do you feel? _____, thank you.
9. This new pen writes _____.
10. It is really a very _____ pen.
11. When you don't feel _____, take a long walk.
    It is often a _____ medicine.
12. We congratulated him on his _____ work.
13. Ray plays tennis _____.
14. His brother is also a _____ tennis player.
15. The movie last night was really _____.
16. She speaks French _____.
17. She is a _____ student of mathematics.
18. Everything that she does, she does _____.
19. Dave dances _____.
20. His sister is also a _____ dancer.
21. I don't understand him _____ when he speaks so rapidly.
22. The weather today is very _____.

General Review

A. *Change the following sentences from affirmative to negative.*

1. They live in Texas.
   (They do not live in Texas. They don't live in Texas.)
2. There are eleven months in a year.
3. The plane arrived at ten o'clock.
4. It is six o'clock now.
5. He went to Chicago by plane.
6. The two boys are in Ms. Collier's office.
7. The magazine cost two dollars.
8. They live in Mexico now.
9. They lived in France for ten years.
10. He got up at five o'clock this morning.
11. They sat in the park for two hours.
12. She speaks English.
13. The meeting begins at nine o'clock.
14. She drinks ten cups of coffee every day.
15. They began to work in June.
16. I am ten years old.
17. They plan to finish the work in July.
18. We got sick last week.
19. The stores were closed because of the holiday.
20. There were four employees absent from work this morning.
21. You usually travel by plane.
22. Mary delivered the merchandise yesterday.
23. Scotty and Karen ate dinner at McDonald's.

B. *Change the sentences in Exercise A to questions.*

1. They live in Texas.
   (Do they live in Texas?)

C. *Change the sentences in Exercise A to questions beginning with a question word.*

1. They live in Texas.
   *(**Where** do they live?   **Why** do they live in Texas?)*

Past Tense
Irregular Verbs

Memorize and practice the past tense forms of these irregular verbs.

become → became	find → found	send → sent
break → broke	forget → forgot	sing → sang
bring → brought	keep → kept	stand → stood
buy → bought	leave → left	take → took
catch → caught	lose → lost	teach → taught
do → did	make → made	think → thought
fight → fought	ring → rang	understand → understood

Supply the correct past tense form of the verbs in parentheses.

1. The plane (leave) Buenos Aires last night at midnight.
   *(The plane **left** Buenos Aires last night at midnight.)*
2. Sue (bring) her cousin to the party last night.
3. I (forget) to bring my notes to the meeting this morning.
4. He (become) president of the company five years ago.
5. We (make) good time on our trip from Houston to Mexico City.
6. I (lose) my book yesterday but (find) it later.
7. The two men (fight) bitterly over the division of the money.
8. The telephone (ring) twice, but no one answered it.
9. The Kanes (send) their three children to summer camp.
10. George (think) about his troubles continuously.
11. Last year Professor Levy (teach) us both English and mathematics.
12. They (buy) the property in 1980 and (sell) it in 1993.
13. Carl (keep) part of the money and (give) the rest to his two brothers.
14. The police (do) their best but never (catch) the real bank robbers.
15. The woman (sing) in French; consequently, we (understand) none of the words.
16. We (stand) on the corner and waited for Mel for two hours.
17. You (break) my stereo, so yesterday I (take) it to the repair shop.

Regular and Irregular Verb Review

The past tense form of regular verbs adds ed *to the simple form.*

> work → worked   study → studied   cry → cried

The past tense form of irregular verbs must be memorized.

> tell → told   go → went   see → saw

Complete the following sentences with the past tense form of the verbs in parentheses.

1. The police (catch) the thief after the robbery.
   *(The police **caught** the thief after the robbery.)*
2. The students _____ (write) the sentences on the blackboard.
3. Edgar _____ (forget) to bring his notes to the meeting.
4. The plane _____ (arrive) an hour late.
5. Gwen _____ (answer) all the doctor's questions.
6. The secretary _____ (make) some mistakes in the letter.
7. The bell _____ (ring) ten minutes ago.
8. I _____ (wait) for Beth for half an hour.
9. The students _____ (go) to this class when the bell _____ (ring).
10. Our new car _____ (cost) more than eight thousand dollars.
11. I _____ (try) to get to work on time yesterday.
12. He _____ (have) a very good time at the picnic.
13. They _____ (plan) to take their vacation in June.
14. Al _____ (take) his vacation in May last year.
15. Amos _____ (send) a present to his mother.
16. Joyce _____ (need) a new umbrella for months; she finally _____ (buy) one last week.
17. The teacher _____ (speak) to the students' parents.
18. He _____ (tell) them that they _____ (have) to study harder.
19. You _____ (break) a lot of dishes last week.
20. I _____ (think) about the problem all night.
21. Mamie Gallagher _____ (be) the president of her company for five years.
22. She _____ (know) the presidents of all the other companies.
23. We _____ (understand) them even when they _____ (speak) rapidly.

Indirect Object
Position

If the indirect object follows the direct object, we use the preposition to or for. If the indirect object precedes the direct object, we do not use a preposition.

He gave the money *to me*.	He gave *me* the money.
I bought a present *for you*.	I bought *you* a present.

A. **Restate the following, putting the indirect object before the direct object.**

1. He sent several letters to her.
   *(He sent **her** several letters.)*
2. She brought the magazines *to me*.
3. She sent flowers *to them*.
4. He told the whole story *to us*.
5. I cooked dinner *for Victoria*.
6. We wrote several letters *to them*.
7. I took the presents *to her*.
8. He sold his property *to a friend*.
9. He gave a piece of the candy *to each child*.
10. Don't show these pictures *to anyone*.
11. He bought several new dresses *for his wife*.
12. They sent some postcards *to us* from South America.

B. **Restate the following, putting the indirect object after the direct object.**

1. She gave me the money.
   *(She gave the money **to me**.)*
2. I sent *her* many presents.
3. Please hand *me* that magazine.
4. Don't tell *her* the rest yet.
5. You made *your sister* a sweater.
6. Don't show *Flo* these things.
7. He wrote *me* a letter on Wednesday.
8. She told *us* the whole story.
9. The teacher gives *us* a lot of homework.
10. You made *me* a promise that you must keep.

Relative Pronouns
Who/Whom, Which, and That

Who *refers to people.* Which *refers to specific animals or things.* That *refers to animals, things, or people as a class. The object (direct or indirect) form of* who *is* whom. *Which* and *that both have the same form whether subject or object.*

> The man *who* called you is here.
> The girl *whom* you saw is my sister.
> To *whom* did you give the key?
> Is this the book *which* you ordered?
> The magazine *which* is on the table is old.
> The Native Americans *that* lived here were called Sioux.
> These are the colors *that* we like.

Complete the following sentences with who, whom, which, *or* that.

1. Was it Jennifer _____ said that?
    *(Was it Jennifer **who** said that?)*
2. This is the report_____ the president wanted.
3. The girls _____ are in my class are all good students.
4. Our teacher, _____ is an American, speaks English perfectly.
5. The car _____ Hernando used belongs to his uncle.
6. The teacher with _____ I studied mathematics last year died last week.
7. To _____ did you sell your furniture?
8. Is this the program _____ you always watch on TV?
9. The movies we saw this summer were all good.
10. These are the kinds of exercises _____ help us learn English.
11. The lamp _____ you broke is my brother's.
12. She is one of the workers _____ went on strike.
13. She was the pilot _____ flew our 747.
14. It is the little things in life_____ count.

To Be

Future Tense with *Will* and *Shall*

The future tense of to be *is* will be *or* shall be. *The contracted form (with 'll) are generally used.*

I shall be (I'll be)	we shall be (we'll be)
you will be (you'll be)	you will be (you'll be)
he will be (he'll be)	
she will be (she'll be)	} they will be (they'll be)
it will be (it'll be)	

Change the following sentences to the future tense with will.

1. I am in the elementary class.
    *(I **shall be** in the elementary class.)*
2. She is our new supervisor.
3. Ms. Koboski and you are in New Orleans.
4. They are both good lawyers.
5. This is your seat.
6. There are two tables in the room.
7. We are very tired after the long drive.
8. I am twenty-five years old.
9. He is angry with us.
10. The dog is happy to see you.
11. Mr. Pate is out of town.
12. Business is very good.
13. The exercises are easy for you.
14. There is no one in the office.
15. The cafeteria is open.
16. We are interested in his progress.
17. You are an English student.
18. The highway is very slippery.

Future Tense

With *Will* and *Shall*

The future tense is formed by using will *or* shall *and the simple form of the verb. The contracted forms (with* 'll*) are generally used.*

I shall go (I'll go)	we shall go (we'll go)
you will go (you'll go)	you will go (you'll go)
he will go (he'll go)	
she will go (she'll go)	they will go (they'll go)
it will go (it'll go)	

Complete the following sentences with the future tense with will *and the verbs in parentheses. Use both the full form and the contracted form.*

1. He _____ (call) you tomorrow.

   *(He **will call** you tomorrow. He'll **call** you tomorrow.)*

2. They _____ (see) us in the morning.

3. I _____ (give) you that money tomorrow.

4. She _____ (help) you with that work.

5. Mary _____ (clean) off the table right away.

6. The stores _____ (close) early today.

7. I _____ (leave) the tip.

8. Helen _____ (find) the book which you need.

9. You _____ (spend) a lot of money there.

10. John _____ (do) well in that job.

11. The wind _____ (blow) that sign down.

12. We _____ (meet) you in Grand Central Station.

13. I _____ (pay) the bill.

14. You _____ (learn) a great deal in that course.

15. We _____ (remain) in Mexico about a month.

Future Tense
Negatives with *Will* and *Shall*

Form the negative of the future tense by placing not *after* will *or* shall. *The contracted form of* will not *is* won't.

I shall not try (I won't try)	we shall not try (we won't try)
you will not try (you won't try)	you will not try (you won't try)
he will not try (he won't try)	
she will not try (she won't try)	they will not try (they won't try)
it will not try (it won't try)	

Change the following sentences from affirmative to negative. Use both the full form and the contracted form.

1. They will arrive on time.
   *(They **will not** arrive on time. They **won't** arrive on time.)*
2. We shall tell Tim about it.
3. I shall be back in an hour.
4. The weather will be cool tomorrow.
5. He will be able to meet us later.
6. These exercises will be easy for you.
7. We shall eat in the same restaurant again.
8. You will get tired of that work.
9. We shall be there before Wednesday.
10. I shall do well in that job.
11. They will sign the contract tomorrow.
12. They will finish the work in April.
13. The meeting will last an hour.
14. The stores will close at noon today.
15. It will cost a lot of money to remodel that house.
16. We shall be ready to leave in an hour.

Future Tense

Questions

Form future tense questions by placing will *before the subject even when a question word is used.*

Will you move? When will you move? Where will you move?

shall I go	shall we go
will you go	will you go
will he go	
will she go	} will they go
will it go	

A. *Change the following sentences to questions.*

1. They'll arrive on Wednesday.
    (**Will** *they arrive on Wednesday?*)
2. I'll be back at three o'clock.
3. The stores will be open until six o'clock.
4. It'll cost $20.75 to fix the lamp.
5. The plant will die because of lack of sunlight.
6. They'll spend two months in France.
7. She'll meet us in the supermarket.
8. They'll pay their bill next week.
9. The meeting will begin at eight o'clock.
10. It'll last an hour.
11. She'll leave a message on the table for him.
12. You'll return in October.
13. There will be three new members in the club.
14. The meeting will be over at three o'clock.
15. They'll write to us on Wednesday.
16. He'll take the children to the park.
17. I'll pass the class.
18. We'll stay in the Hotel Americana.

B. *Change the sentences in Exercise A to questions beginning with question words.*

1. They'll arrive on Wednesday.
    (**When will** *they arrive?*)

Prepositions

Complete the following sentences with an appropriate preposition.

1. This book belongs _____ Theodore.
   *(This book belongs **to** Theodore.)*
2. We all went _____ a walk _____ the park.
3. We bought this car _____ August.
4. We plan to trade it _____ a new one _____ the spring.
5. We looked everywhere _____ the pen which Guy lost.
6. Nan usually sits _____ this desk.
7. I make a lot of errors _____ spelling.
8. The man walked quickly _____ the room and sat down.
9. She spends a lot _____ time _____ her English.
10. We read _____ the accident _____ the newspaper this morning.
11. I must write a letter _____ my aunt.
12. She went _____ the corner store _____ some groceries.
13. Lea sits _____ front _____ me at the meeting.
14. The boat moved slowly _____ the coast.
15. Everyone laughed _____ William's story.
16. The woman smiled _____ me pleasantly.
17. He thanked me _____ my interest _____ the matter.
18. How much did they pay _____ their new home?
19. They buy everything _____ credit.
20. They told me all _____ their trip _____ South America.
21. He left the office _____ once, as soon as he heard _____ the accident.
22. Please pick _____ those papers which are _____ the floor.
23. He never comes _____ club meetings _____ time.
24. We live a long way _____ the airport.
25. What time do you get _____ every morning?

Infinitives

Use infinitives to complete the meaning of various verbs.

> He wants *to see you.*
> We tried *to call you.*

Use infinitives to complete the meaning of various adjectives and adverbs.

> These exercises are easy *to do.*
> It was impossible *to open* that door.

Use infinitives either alone or after in order *to express the idea of purpose.*

> He went there *to see* his friend.
> We came early *in order to get* good seats.

Using infinitive constructions, complete the following sentences in your own words.

For example: I'll be glad _____
        (I'll be glad to help you with your homework.)

1. He went here in order _____.
2. She wants _____.
3. I prefer _____.
4. It is easy_____.
5. We hope _____.
6. They are afraid _____.
7. You went there _____.
8. You went there in order _____.
9. I forgot _____.
10. It was impossible _____.
11. We both like _____.
12. You ought _____.
13. I told him _____.
14. You don't want _____.
15. It is hard _____.
16. They expect _____.
17. It is possible _____.
18. We are too weak _____.
19. I know how _____.
20. Did you forget _____?

It Takes

It takes *expresses a period of time which is necessary in order to complete some action.* It takes *is always followed by an infinitive.*

> *It takes me* 45 minutes to get ready in the morning. (Present)
> *It took us* three weeks to finish the project. (Past)
> *It will (It'll)* take you a half-hour to change that tire. (Future)

Change each of the following sentences so that it begins with a present tense, past tense, or future tense form of it takes *as required by the meaning.*

1. She walked to work in ten minutes.

   (***It took** her ten minutes to walk to work.*)

2. I finished my work in an hour.

3. She learned to speak English well in only one year.

4. I wrote my paper in thirty minutes.

5. The train went around the mountain in three hours.

6. They finished the bridge in one year.

7. The cable reached him in two days.

8. We walk to school every morning in about fifteen minutes.

9. You'll get there in about an hour.

10. We'll paint the bathroom in two hours.

11. You'll paint the kitchen in only 1.5 hours.

12. I wash and dress each morning in less than fifteen minutes.

13. The clown puts on his makeup in half an hour.

14. He learned to swim in just a few days.

15. She recovered from her illness in two months.

16. I'll run to the corner store and get what you need in just two or three minutes.

Past Tense
Irregular Verbs

Memorize and practice the past tense forms of these irregular verbs.

blow → blew	hurt → hurt	shoot → shot
cut → cut	lend → lent	shut → shut
drive → drove	mean → meant	sleep → slept
fall → fell	meet → met	spend → spent
find → found	pay → paid	steal → stole
fly → flew	ride → rode	throw → threw
grow → grew	say → said	win → won
hit → hit	run → ran	wake → woke
hold → held	shake → shook	wear → wore

Complete the following sentences with the past tense form of the irregular verbs in parentheses.

1. Charles _____ (fall) from his bike and hurt his arm.
   *(Charles **fell** from his bike and hurt his arm.)*
2. I _____ (pay) six dollars for this book.
3. We _____ (shake) hands and then _____ (say) good night.
4. The force of the wind was so great that it _____ (blow) down several trees in our yard.
5. The pitcher _____ (throw) a slow ball and the batter _____ (hit) it for a home run.
6. I _____ (sleep) very well last night.
7. We _____ (meet) Ivy on the corner of Oak Avenue.
8. She finally _____ (find) her lost book.
9. Alma _____ (wear) her new silk dress to the party last night.
10. The drunken driver first _____ (cut) in front of us and then _____ (run) his car over the curb.
11. We _____ (drive) to Washington in Noel's new car.
12. He _____ (hold) the bird in his hand for several minutes.
14. Our team _____ (win) the first game but _____ (lose) the second.
15. We _____ (shut) all the windows and _____ (lock) all the doors before we _____ (go) out.
16. We rented two horses and _____ (ride) all around the park on horseback.

Present Continuous Tense

*Form the present continuous tense by placing the appropriate form of to be before the present participle (*ing *form) of the main verb. The contracted forms are generally used.*

I am working	we are working
you are working	you are working
he is working	
she is working	they are working
it is working	

The present continuous tense describes an action that is going on at the present moment.

He *is talking* with her now.
It*'s raining.*

Complete the following sentences with the present continuous tense form of the verbs in parentheses.

1. They _____ (wait) for us on the corner now.
   *(They're **waiting** for us on the corner now.)*
2. The bus _____ (stop) for us now.
3. Listen! I think the telephone _____ (ring).
4. I see that you _____ (wear) your new suit today.
5. Look! It _____ (begin) to rain.
6. Listen! Someone _____ (knock) at the door.
7. Please be quiet! The baby _____ (sleep).
8. Look! The cat _____ (try) to climb that tall tree.
9. Janet _____ (do) well in her studies.
10. The leaves _____ (begin) to fall from the trees.
11. John _____ (have) lunch in the cafeteria now.
12. Listen! That's Eve who _____ (play) the piano.
13. At present they _____ (travel) in South America.
14. For the time being, Mr. Collins _____ (act) as manager of this department.
15. All the big stores _____ (have) sales this month.
16. They stole a plane and now they _____ (fly) out of the country.
17. We _____ (grow) a lot of large tomatoes this year.
18. We _____ (do) an exercise right now.

Present Continuous Tense

Note the difference between the simple present tense and the present continuous tense. The present tense describes actions that occur every day or all the time, while the present continuous tense describes actions that are happening now.

> Peter talks to Anne all the time.   (Present)
> Peter is talking to Anne at this moment.   (Present Continuous)

Supply the simple present tense or the present continuous tense as required by the meaning of the sentence.

1. Mr. Hansen often _____ (travel) to Atlanta on business.
   *(Mr. Hansen often **travels** to Atlanta on business.)*
2. Our club _____ (meet) two times every week.
3. Mr. Cole _____ (teach) us at present. He _____ (substitute) for Mr. Russell, who is our regular teacher.
4. Every hour our churchbell _____ (ring). Listen! I believe it _____ (ring) now.
5. Stella _____ (watch) TV now. I believe that she always _____ (watch) a show at this time.
6. Listen! Someone _____ (knock) at the door.
7. Jay never _____ (come) to work on time.
8. At this moment I _____ (read) sentence number 8 in the exercise.
9. The wind always _____ (blow) hard in this section of town.
10. For the time being, while Mr. Press is away, Ms. Brennan _____ (acts) as manager of our department.
11. Klein's _____ (have) a big sale on shoes today.
12. Kurt seems to be very busy. I guess he _____ (study) for his science test.
13. I _____ (get) up at seven o'clock every morning.
14. Ed usually _____ (stay) in a hotel when he _____ (come) to town, but tonight he _____ (stay) with us.
15. The sun always _____ (rise) in the east. Look! It _____ (rise) now.
16. Mr. and Mrs. Bush _____ (build) a new home on Hollywood Boulevard.

Present Continuous Tense
Negatives and Questions

Form present continuous tense negatives by placing not *after the auxiliary* to be. *The contracted forms are generally used.*

> She is studying English
> She is *not* studying English.   She *isn't* studying English.

Form present continuous tense questions by placing the to be *auxiliary before the subject.*

> They are working.   *Are* they working?

A. *Change the following sentences from affirmative to negative.*

1. The telephone is ringing.
    *(The telephone **is not** ringing. The telephone **isn't** ringing.)*
2. It is beginning to rain.
3. The sky is getting very dark.
4. She is working on the fourth floor at present.
5. The maid is cleaning the room now.
6. They are taking a walk in the park.
7. You are having lunch outside.
8. John is doing well in his studies at present.
9. We are laughing at what you said.
10. They are traveling in Europe at present.
11. I am taking dancing lessons.
12. The leaves are beginning to fall from the trees.
13. All the birds are flying south.
14. Ellen is writing a series of articles on the economic situation.
15. They are planning to leave for Spain soon.
16. He is looking for the key which he lost.

B. *Change the sentences from Exercise A to questions.*

1. The telephone is ringing.
    (Is the telephone ringing?)

Contractions

Affirmative

These contracted forms are used more frequently than their full forms in spoken English.

I am → I'm	they are → they're	we shall → we'll
you are → you're	I shall → I'll	they will → they'll
he is → he's	you will → you'll	there is → there's
she is → she's	he will → he'll	there are → there're
it is → it's	she will → she'll	
we are → we're	it will → it'll	

Note that the following types of contractions with objects or proper nouns as subjects of the sentence appear in spoken English but generally not in written English.

The telephone is ringing.	The telephone's ringing.
The Reagans are on vacation.	The Reagans're on vacation.

Give the contracted forms of the verbs in these sentences.

1. She is a good employee.
   (**She's** *a good employee.*)
2. They are waiting for us on the tenth floor.
3. I shall be back before noon.
4. She is very busy.
5. It is raining hard.
6. She will surely finish the work today.
7. We are old friends.
8. They are planning to leave next week.
9. It is almost three o'clock.
10. We are coming next Friday.
11. You will lose my keys if you play with them.
12. It is just leaving the station now.
13. There is someone at the door.
14. They will remain in Europe all summer.
15. He is a big boy for his age.
16. You are very kind to say that.
17. I am glad that you were able to come.
18. There is nothing to do now.
19. He will know the answer.
20. It will be winter soon.

Contractions
Negative

These contracted forms are used more frequently than their full forms in spoken English.

are not → aren't	do not → don't
is not → isn't	does not → doesn't
was not → wasn't	did not → didn't
were not → weren't	will not → won't

Use the contracted forms of these negative verbs.

1. He did not come to the meeting yesterday.
   *(He **didn't** come to the meeting yesterday.)*
2. They do not speak English well.
3. She is not studying science at present.
4. He is not a good manager.
5. They are not satisfied with their new apartment.
6. He does not appreciate your help.
7. You did not talk to the manager.
8. She does not spend much money on entertainment.
9. You are not the only person who feels that way about Melissa.
10. We were not pleased with the results of our examinations.
11. George was not at the meeting last night.
12. She and her husband do not get along well.
13. I shall not be back before six.
14. There were not many employees absent from work today.
15. They will not leave for Europe before next month.
16. You are not doing that exercise correctly.
17. There are not any good shows on television tonight.

Articles

A and an are indefinite articles. They refer to objects that have not been specifically identified.

> *A* book is on the table.

The is a definite article. It refers to a particular object.

> *The* book that I am reading is on the table.

Complete the following sentences with the correct article.

1. _____ chair you are sitting in is very comfortable.
   (***The** chair you are sitting in is very comfortable.*)
2. There is _____ pencil (no particular pencil) on the desk.
3. There is _____ customer (no particular customer) outside who wishes to see Mrs. Winston.
4. _____ customer whom Mr. Garp telephoned this morning is here now.
5. I want to find _____ good book (no particular book) to read tonight.
6. _____ book which I am reading now belongs to Leslie.
7. _____ book which gave me the greatest pleasure was *Les Misérables*.
8. _____ good book (any good book) is always a pleasure for me.
9. _____ dog which Judy is walking has long ears.
11. I must buy _____ new briefcase. (At this point I have no particular briefcase in mind.)
12. _____ new briefcase which I bought yesterday is made of leather. (It is now a definite briefcase.)
13. Pete bought _____ new hat yesterday in Macy's. (As yet no definite hat.)
14. _____ hat which Pete bought in Macy's yesterday (now a definite hat) arrived this afternoon.
15. I also bought _____ new hat in Macy's yesterday.
    (Though perhaps a definite hat to me, it is still not a definite hat to my listener.)

Articles

1.   The indefinite article (a or an) is used only with singular nouns.

There is a *book* on the table.   There are *books* on the table.

The definite article (the) is used with both singular and plural nouns.

The *book* that I am reading is on the table.

The *books* that I am reading are on the table.

2.   Nouns of indefinite quantity or quality do not take an article.

Gold is an important metal.   *Honesty* is the best policy.

When such nouns are used to indicate a particular quality or quantity, they should be preceded by the.

The *gold* in this ring is very old.

The *honesty* of this man is above question.

3.   No article is used before the name of persons, countries, streets, cities or towns when they are used as proper nouns.

They live in Northbrook on Whitehall Court.

Ms. Draper is going to Czechoslovakia.

If such words are used as adjectives, they are preceded by an article.

Chicago is a large city.

The Chicago fire was very interesting.

Broadway is very interesting.

The Broadway merchants held a meeting.

Names of rivers, seas, mountain chains, and countries are preceded by the when they contain an adjective or some qualifying word.

the Mississippi River   *the* Ural Mountains

the Pacific Ocean   *the* United States

4.   No article is used when a noun is modified by someone's name.

Nancy's book   Pope John Paul's speech

No article is used when a noun is modified by a possessive pronoun.

his hat   my book

Articles

A. *Some of the blank spaces below require articles; others do not. Fill in the articles where needed.*

1. _____ fresh air is needed by all growing children.
   (Fresh air is needed by all growing children.)
2. _____ air in this room is not fresh.
3. _____ telephone rings very often in our office.
4. I always get on _____ bus at _____ same corner every morning.
5. Look! Lou is waving to us from across _____ street.
6. _____ some women from _____ Peru visited us.
7. _____ tea will not keep you awake at night.
8. However, _____ coffee seems to keep some people awake.
9. _____ tea in this pot is very weak.
10. _____ coffee which comes from Latin America is _____ best in _____ world.
11. _____ cotton is one of _____ most important products of _____ South.
12. The U.S. Constitution guarantees _____ right to free speech.
13. Some of _____ important products which we import from _____ India are _____ tea, _____ cotton, and _____ rice.
14. _____ copper is _____ good conductor of _____ electricity.
15. Plenty of _____ rain and _____ sun are necessary for _____ raising of _____ cotton.
16. _____ sun is shining now, but part of _____ sky is still dark.
17. At times everyone must take _____ medicine.
18. _____ medicine which _____ doctor prescribed helped my cough.
19. He likes to study _____ history.
20. In that course, we study _____ history of all _____ western European countries.
21. _____ milk is my daughter's favorite drink.
22. I spilled _____ milk which was on the table.
23. When you go to the store, please buy some _____ milk.

Articles

B. *Some of the sentences require articles; others do not. Fill in the articles as required.*

1. We went to _____ Chicago this summer.
    (We went to Chicago this summer.)

2. When you go to _____ Chicago, be sure to visit _____ Sears Building.

3. She works in _____ building on _____ corner of Fifth Avenue and 72nd Street.

4. New York City is _____ largest city in _____ United States.

5. _____ traffic on _____ Madison Avenue is very heavy.

6. _____ Pittsburgh is _____ center of _____ steel industry of _____ Pennsylvania.

7. _____ Hudson River forms _____ boundary between _____ New York State and _____ New Jersey.

8. _____ Middle East is rich in _____ natural resources.

9. On our trip to _____ South America, we plan to stop off at _____ Haiti and _____ Dominican Republic.

10. _____ Great Wall of China is visible from outer space.

11. _____ rivers of _____ eastern part of _____ United States flow toward _____ Atlantic Ocean.

12. _____ machines which we ordered from _____ Pittsburgh arrived this morning.

13. The distance from _____ Washington, D.C., to _____ Minneapolis is about one thousand miles.

14 _____ largest river in _____ Germany is _____ Rhine.

15. _____ Mexico City subways are very quiet.

16. _____ Bering Strait was once _____ land mass.

17. _____ climate of _____ southern Italy is very warm.

Articles

C. *Fill in the articles where needed.*

1. _____ chair on which you are sitting is uncomfortable.
   (***The** chair on which you are sitting is uncomfortable.*)

2. _____ fire which destroyed _____ building started on _____ roof.

3. My family bought _____ new stove last week. It has _____ timer, _____ clock, and _____ light for_____ oven.

4. The man took _____ his pages and put them into _____ briefcase.

5. I enjoyed _____ speech by _____ Mr. Chin last night. He spoke about _____ life in _____ China.

6. We all had _____ good time at _____ dance last night.

7. _____ price of _____ gold is rising, but _____ price of _____ silver is falling.

8. Much of _____ silver which we use in _____ United States comes from _____ Montana.

9. _____ drinking water often varies in taste, according to locality. _____ drinking water in New York City is very good.

10. There are _____ several new magazines on _____ table in _____ hall.

11. We often go to _____ zoo and watch _____ animals.

12. _____ candidates for mayor debated _____ crime problem.

13. Please open _____ windows. _____ air in this room is not good.

14. They plan to visit _____ Russia this summer. I understand _____ Russian language is difficult to learn.

15. Mr. and Mrs. Ames are now traveling in _____ South America. They plan to visit _____ Venezuela, _____ Colombia, _____ Peru, and _____ Argentina.

16. They will arrive in _____ Caracas around noon.

Going To
Future Tense

Another way (in addition to shall/will + *the simple form of the verb) to express the future tense is to use the appropriate form of* to be going to *and the simple form of the verb. The contracted forms are generally used.*

I am (I'm) going to see	we are (we're) going to see
you are (you're) going to see	you are (you're) going to see
he is (he's) going to see	
she is (she's) going to see	they are (they're) going to see
it is (it's) going to see	

Complete the following sentences with the going to *form of the future tense, using the verbs in parentheses. Use both the full form and the contracted form.*

1. They _____ (visit) us next weekend.
   (They are going to visit us next weekend.
   They're going to visit us next weekend.)
2. We _____ (eat) out tonight.
3. I _____ (leave) for Europe on Tuesday.
4. They _____ (wait) for us after the show.
5. We _____ (get) up early tomorrow morning and go fishing.
6. She _____ (drive) to California.
7. We _____ (go) to Canada on our vacation.
8. You _____ (have) an exam in mathematics tomorrow.
9. They _____ (go) to Europe by plane.
10. Mike _____ (take) Alex to the dance tonight.
11. It _____ (be) difficult to reach him at this late hour.
12. I believe it _____ (rain).
13. Henry _____ (study) to be a doctor.
14. You _____ (stay) home tonight and watch television.
15. Mr. and Mrs. Blake _____ (build) a summer home on Merritt Island.
16. He _____ (start) his new job next week.
17. They _____ (move) the plant to the suburbs.
18. It _____ (be) another warm day.

Going To
Past Tense

The past form of going to *indicates an action which was planned or intended but which did not happen. Use the appropriate past tense form of* to be going to *and the simple form of the verb.*

I was going to speak	we were going to speak
you were going to speak	you were going to speak
he was going to speak	
she was going to speak	they were going to speak
it was going to speak	

Substitute the past tense form of going to *for the verbs in italics.*

1. I *intended* to do it yesterday, but I was too busy.
    (***I was going** to do it yesterday, but I was too busy.*)

2. We *intended* to go swimming, but the weather was too cold.

3. I *planned* to spend the evening on my homework but fell asleep right after dinner.

4. They *intended* to spend the whole year in Europe, but their money ran out.

5. We *planned* to go by car but finally decided to go by plane.

6. You *planned* to give a big reception but then decided against it.

7. They *planned* to get married in June but then waited until October.

8. At first he *intended* to ask Sally to the dance, but finally he invited Jane.

9. I *intended* to rewrite my exercises but didn't have enough time.

10. I *planned* to return your book today but left it at home.

11. They *planned* to leave for Europe last week, but Mrs. Thompson was too ill to go.

12. At first she *intended* to put the boy in the elementary class, but later she put him in an advanced section.

13. We *planned* to go to a movie last night but were too tired.

14. I *intended* to write to you several times, but something always interfered.

Present Continuous Tense
Future Time

The present continuous tense of verbs like come, leave, arrive, return, *and* go *is often used to describe future action. An adverb of time usually accompanies such usage.*

> She *is leaving* for Moscow next week.
> They *are returning* to their homelands when the semester ends.

Complete the following sentences by using the present continuous tense of the verbs in parentheses.

1. When _____ you _____ (leave) for Rome?
   I hear that Charlene _____ (leave) next Saturday.
   *(When **are you leaving** for Rome? I hear that Charlene **is leaving** next Saturday.)*

2. My brother _____ (come) to visit me next week.

3. What time _____ you _____ (go) to the movies tonight? Ron says that he _____ (go) at nine o'clock.

4. Coretta _____ (sail) for England on the Queen Elizabeth II Saturday.

5. When _____ Ms. Green _____ (come) to see you?

6. Tony says that he _____ (leave) for San Antonio on the fifteenth.

7. I _____ (go) to the seashore on my vacation.

8. Mr. Schwartz _____ (arrive) on Pan Am Flight 109 this evening.

9. Where _____ you _____ (go) on your vacation? _____ your wife _____ (go) with you?

10. Mr. Zane _____ (leave) for Utah in the morning.

11. Some friends _____ (come) to visit us tonight.

12. She _____ (go) to Denver on Wednesday, but her husband _____ not _____ (go) until next week.

13. On what bus _____ your friend _____ (arrive)?

14. He _____ (come) in on a Trailways bus which arrives at eight o'clock.

15. Mr. Wyler _____ (fly) to Dallas on Saturday.

16. I _____ (leave) for Houston in the morning.

17. On what train _____ Mr. North _____ (leave)?

Auxiliary Verbs
Negatives

Auxiliary verbs such as can, may, must, *and* should *accompany main verbs. Form their negatives by placing* not *after the auxiliaries. The contracted forms* can't, mustn't, *and* shouldn't *are generally used, but note that no contraction is used with* may.

> She can speak English.
> She can*not* speak English.   She *can't* speak English.

> We must go there.
> We must *not* go there.   We *mustn't* go there.

Change the following sentences from affirmative to negative. Use both the full form and the contracted form (except for may).

1. We can meet you later.
    *(We **cannot** meet you later. We **can't** meet you later.)*
2. You may sit here.
3. We should tell her about it.
4. He may leave on Wednesday.
5. They can go by plane.
6. We must wait here.
7. I can understand him easily.
8. She should sit near the window.
9. We must do the same thing again.
10. She can play the piano well.
11. He can understand everything I say.
12 You should watch television every night.
13. She may pass her examination.
14. You can see him later.
15. You may fish here.

Auxiliary Verbs
Questions

Form questions with auxiliary verbs by placing the auxiliary before the subject.

She can speak English.	*Can she* speak English?
We should go there.	*Should we* go there?

Change the following statements to questions.

1. They should obey the rules.
   (Should they obey the rules?)
2. They both can speak English well.
3. Betsy should spend more time on her English.
4. We may sit in these chairs.
5. They can meet us at two o'clock.
6. I may call you later.
7. He should eat less meat.
8. He may tell her.
9. We should speak to her about it.
10. They may leave now.
11. You could go by plane.
12. You could send them a cable.
13. I should stay at home more.
14. Allan may wait in his office.
15. Al can go with us to the beach.
16. She could leave immediately.

Auxiliary Verbs
Questions

With both auxiliary verbs and to be we form questions by placing the auxiliary or to be before the subject. This rule applies even when the question begins with words like where, when, why, how, or what.

They should go home now.	*Should* they go home now?
He is in Chicago.	*Is* he in Chicago?
When *should* they go home?	Where *is* he?

Change the following sentences to questions beginning with the question words in parentheses.

1. He can see her later. (When)
   *(**When** can he see her?)*
2. The babysitter could wait here. (Where)
3. You may study here. (Where)
4. He is very sick. (How sick)
5. I can understand English very well. (How well)
6. You should be here at three o'clock. (What time)
7. We should tell her about it. (Why)
8. He can meet us in the store. (Where)
9. Lew is six feet tall. (How tall)
10. They are in the cafeteria. (Where)
11. I should tell her the truth. (Why)
12. You must be here at one o'clock. (What time)
13. Karen should sit near the blackboard. (Where)
14. He is a very serious person. (What kind of person)
15. It is three o'clock. (What time)
16. Both engineers are absent from work today. (Why!)

Short Answers

Short answers are the most common way of answering direct questions. A short answer consists of the subject of the sentence and an auxiliary verb or part of to be. *Note that if there is no auxiliary verb in an expected answer, the verb* to do *is used.*

Can you play the piano?	Yes, I can.	No, I can't.
Does she know the answer?	Yes, she does.	No, she doesn't.
Are they coming?	Yes, they are.	No, they aren't.

Pronouns generally replace nouns in short answers.

Will Ms. Wong be here soon?	Yes, she will.	No, she won't.
Did it rain yesterday?	Yes, it did.	No, it didn't.

A. Give affirmative short answers to these questions.

1. Can you speak Spanish?
   (Yes, I can.)
2. Do you live in Maine?
3. Does your teacher speak Russian?
4. Does your teacher live in Florida?
5. Will you be in class tomorrow?
6. Will Ali be in class, too?
7. Are you going out tonight?
8. Is it raining now?
9. Does it often rain in Oregon?
10. Is the lesson over?
11. Is the time up?
12. Did you study your lesson?
13. Did you go to the movies last night?
14. Is the weather warm today?
15. Was it warm yesterday?
16. Did your friend visit you last night?
17. Is today Friday?
18. Was yesterday Thursday?
19. Will tomorrow be Sunday?
20. May I open the window?
21. Can you fly an airplane?
22. Did it rain yesterday?
23. Did you study yesterday?
24. Were you busy yesterday?
25. Will you be busy tomorrow?
26. Is Washington a beautiful city?

B. Give negative short answers to the questions in A.

1. Can you speak Spanish?   *(No, I can't.)*

Adverbs and Adjectives
Comparative Form

The comparative form of one-syllable adjectives and adverbs adds er.

cold → cold*er*	soon → soon*er*
smart → smart*er*	fast → fast*er*

The comparative form of adjectives and adverbs of more than two syllables usually uses more.

difficult → *more difficult*	quickly → *more quickly*
beautiful → *more beautiful*	carefully → *more carefully*

Some adjectives and adverbs are irregular.

good → *better*	well → *better*
bad → *worse*	badly → *worse*

The comparative form of adjectives and adverbs is followed by than.

She is *taller than* her sister.
He drives *more carefully than* his brother [does].

A. *Complete these sentences by supplying the comparative form of the adjective or adverb in parentheses. Be sure to include the word* than.

1. He is _____ (young) _____ I [am].
   *(He is **younger than** I am.)*
2. Carmen is much _____ (old) _____ expected.
3. Alaska is _____ (big) _____ Delaware.
4. This book is _____ (good) _____ the last one we used.
5. The weather this winter is _____ (bad) _____ the weather last winter.
6. This exercise is _____ (easy) _____ the last one.
7. This metal is _____ (valuable) _____ gold.
8. Jane is_____ (attractive) _____ her sister.
9. He goes there _____ (often) _____ I.
10. They go to the movies _____ (frequent) _____ you.
11. I get up every morning much _____ (early) _____ you.

Adverbs and Adjectives
Comparative Form

B. Complete these sentences by supplying the comparative form
    of the adjectives or adverbs in parentheses. Be sure to include
    the word than.

1. She speaks _____ (rapid) _____ I.
    *(She speaks **more rapidly than I**.)*

2. He prepares his homework _____ (careful) _____ most
    students.

3. She works _____ (hard) _____ her sister.

4. We stayed _____ (long) _____ we expected.

5. Our troops fought _____ (brave) _____ anyone expected.

6. The time passed _____ (quick) _____ I expected.

7. The speaker spoke _____ (loud) _____ was really necessary.

8. They arrived _____ (soon) _____ we.

9. The weather today is _____ (warm) _____ the weather
    yesterday.

10. John's car was much _____ (expensive) _____ my car.

11. This contract is _____ (satisfactory) _____ the previous one.

12. This street is even _____ (wide) _____ the highway.

13. These exercises are _____ (difficult) _____ some of the others.

14. The climate of Caracas is _____ (good) _____ that of
    Maracaibo.

15. Lil is much _____ (clever) _____ her brother.

16. This summer is _____ (hot) _____ last summer.

17. She spoke _____ (rapid) _____ expected.

Adverbs and Adjectives
Superlative Form

The superlative form of one-syllable adjectives and adverbs adds est.

cold → cold*est*	soon → soon*est*
smart → smart*est*	fast → fast*est*

The superlative form of adjectives and adverbs of more than one syllable usually uses most.

difficult → most difficult	quickly → most quickly
beautiful → most beautiful	carefully → most carefully

Some adjectives and adverbs are irregular.

good → best	well → best
bad → worst	badly → worst

The superlative form of all adjectives and adverbs is preceded by the.

She is *the tallest* girl in the class.
He drives *the most carefully* of anyone in the family.

Supply the superlative form of the adjective or adverb in parentheses. Be sure to use the word the.

1. She speaks _____ (rapidly) of any of my friends.
   *(She speaks **the most rapidly** of any of my friends.)*
2. This is _____ (expensive) book that I own.
3. George is _____ (bad) student in the class.
4. The *Herald* is_____ (important) newspaper in the town.
5. Robin works _____ (hard) of all the ballerinas in the troupe.
6. He is _____ (ambitious) man that I know.
7. Of the three brothers, Malcolm wakes up _____ .
8. Rebecca swims _____ (gracefully) of all the team members.
9. She is _____ (intelligent) person that I know.
10. The story which you told was _____ (funny) of all.
11. January is _____ (cold) month of the year.
12. Which is _____ (good) route from Miami to New York?

Past Continuous Tense

Form the past continuous tense with the past tense of to be *and the present participle of the main verb.*

I was working	we were working
you were working	you were working
he was working	
she was working	} they were working
it was working	

The past continuous tense describes a past action which was going on when another action took place.

> I *was sleeping* when you called.
> They *were eating* dinner when we arrived.

A. Supply the correct past continuous tense form of the verbs in parentheses.

1. They _____ (eat) in the restaurant on the corner when I saw them.
    *(They **were eating** in the restaurant on the corner when I saw them.)*

2. It _____ (rain) when I left home.

3. When you telephoned, I _____ (have) dinner.

4. They _____ (travel) in Europe when they heard the news.

5. The baby _____ (sleep) soundly when I went to wake him.

6. He _____ just _____ (order) breakfast when I went to his hotel room.

7. I got sick while we _____ (drive) to my grandmother's.

8. He _____ (work) in California when his father died.

9. I _____ just _____ (take) a nap when you called.

10. She _____ (talk) with Mr. Samuels when I saw her in the hall.

11. The accident happened while they _____ (travel) in Greece.

12. The flight attendant fell as she _____ (get) into a taxi.

13. The car _____ (travel) at high speed when it approached the corner.

Past Continuous Tense

B. *In the following sentences, supply the past tense or the past continuous tense form of the verbs in parentheses as required by the meaning.*

1. I _____ (study) very diligently last night.
   *(I **studied** very diligently last night.)*
2. I _____ (study) last night when you called me on the.phone.
   *(I **was studying** last night when you called me on the phone.)*
3. While I _____ (go) home last night, I saw a bad accident.
4. I _____ (go) home last night by bus.
5. We _____ (drive) to an amusement park yesterday.
6. We _____ (drive) at about forty miles an hour when the accident happened.
7. We _____ (have) our dinner when you phoned.
8. We _____ (have) our dinner in a restaurant last night.
9. While I _____ (come) to work this morning, I met an old friend.
10. I _____ (come) to work in a taxi this morning.
11. The wind _____ (blow) hard when I came to work this morning.
12. The wind _____ (blow) hard this morning.
13. It _____ (rain) hard last night.
14. It _____ (rain) hard when I left the office at five o'clock.
15. The sun _____ (shine) brightly when I got up this morning.
16. The sun _____ (shine) brightly this morning.
17. At seven o'clock, when you telephoned, I _____ (read) the newspaper.
18. I _____ (read) two books last week.
19. I _____ (sleep) soundly when the phone rang.
20. I _____ (sleep) soundly last night.
21. June _____ (play) the piano when I arrived.

Past Continuous Tense

C. *Supply either the past tense or the past continuous tense of the verbs in parentheses as required by the meaning.*

1. As I _____ (walk) home yesterday, I _____ (meet) a blind woman who _____ (ask) me for directions to the subway.
   (*As I **was walking** home yesterday, I **met** a blind woman who **asked** me for directions to the subway.*)

2. It _____ (rain) hard when I _____ (leave) home this morning.

3. Pete _____ (fall) and _____ (hurt) himself when he _____ (ride) his bicycle yesterday.

4. At five o'clock, when I _____ (call) the Kennedy's home, they _____ (have) dinner.

5. When the oil embargo _____ (start), Sophia _____ (live) in Switzerland.

6. We _____ (sit) on our front porch when Ms. Gold _____ (drive) up in her new car.

7. As Terri _____ (get) out of the taxi, she _____ (slip) and _____ (break) her leg.

8. Mr. Cash _____ (drive) at about forty miles an hour when the accident _____ (happen).

9. Your telegram _____ (come) just as I _____ (leave) my home.

10. Last night, just as we _____ (leave) for the movies, some friends _____ (call) on us.

11. Nelson _____ (talk) with his boss when I last _____ (see) him.

12. At noon, when you _____ (telephone), I _____ (work) in my garden.

Past Continuous Tense

D. *Change each of the following sentences from the past tense to the past continuous tense. Add any words, phrases, or clauses which you may need in order to complete the meaning of the sentence.*

1. I studied my English lesson last night.
    (*I **was studying** my English lesson last night **when my friend called me**.*)
2. I talked to Maurice Cooper this morning.
3. Tony walked home from work yesterday afternoon.
4. She ate her dinner.
5. I finished my work.
6. Larry spoke to Ms. Watkins about a raise.
7. I wrote a letter last night.
8. He lived in Africa.
9. They got off the bus at Broad Street.
10. We had lunch with Mr. and Mrs. Chambers.
11. Chris left home this morning.
12. Dr. Berger had a haircut.
13. Sharon wrote her term paper on a computer.
14. I visited the Andersons.
15. The puppy cried.

Future Continuous Tense

Form the future continuous tense by using shall be or will be and the present participle of the main verb. The contracted forms are generally used.

Singular:	I shall be working	(I'll be working)
	you will be working	(you'll be working)
	he will be working	(he'll be working)
	she will be working	(she'll be working)
	it will be working	(it'll be working)

Plural:	we shall be working	(we'll be working)
	you will be working	(you'll be working)
	they will be working	(they'll be working)

The future continuous tense describes an action that will be going on when another action takes place.

I *shall be studying* when you return this evening.
They'*ll be traveling* in Germany by the time you arrive here.

Supply the future continuous tense of the verbs in parentheses.

1. If you come at noon, we _____ (eat) lunch.
   *(If you come at noon, **we'll be eating** lunch.)*
2. At this time next month, we _____ (travel) in South America.
3. At ten o'clock tomorrow morning, I _____ (have) my music lesson.
4. I _____ (wait) on the corner for you at the usual time.
5. If you call her at six, she probably _____ (practice) the piano.
6. It probably _____ (rain) when you get back.
7. If you come before six, I_____ (work) in my garden.
8. Tomorrow afternoon at this time, we _____ (fly) over the Caribbean.
9. Don't call him after seven. He _____ (watch) his favorite television program.
10. Don't call her now. She _____ (take) her usual afternoon nap.
11. At this time next year, he _____ (study) at the University of Illinois.

Much, Many, A Lot Of

Much *is used with non-countable nouns; that is, things that cannot be counted and do not add s to show plurality.*

These nouns do not normally have plural forms.

much sugar	*much* rain	*much* coffee

Many *is used with plural countable nouns.*

many cups of sugar	*many* cans of coffee
many students	*many* books

A lot of *is used interchangeably with* much *and* many. A lot of *is the most commonly used term of these three.*

a lot of sugar	*a lot of* books	*a lot of* love

A. *Complete the following sentences with* much *or* many.

1. There aren't _____ large factories in this town.
   *(There aren't **many** large factories in this town.)*
2. He doesn't spend _____ time on his English.
3. Does this factory produce _____ different kinds of products?
4. Does she spend _____ money on clothes?
5. Is there _____ oil in Venezuela?
6. He doesn't drink _____ milk.
7. Does he have _____ friends in this office?
8. There aren't _____ mountains in that part of the country.
9. There isn't _____ milk in this pitcher.
10. How _____ time do you spend on your English every day?
11. How _____ windows are there in your office?
12. How _____ times a week do you go to the movies?
13. How _____ money do you spend on magazines each month?
14. He doesn't make _____ mistakes in spelling.
15. There isn't _____ snow on the ground.
16. She doesn't drink _____ coffee.
17. How _____ cups of coffee do you drink every day?
18. There weren't _____ employees absent yesterday.

B. *In which of the sentences in Exercise A can you substitute* a lot of *for* much *or* many?

Also, Too, Either

Also *and* too *change to* either *in negative sentences.*

> I want to come too.
> I don't want to come *either.*

> They also want this book.
> They don't want this book *either.*

A. Change the following sentences from affirmative to negative.

1. Mary likes to study with our group, too.
   *(Mary doesn't like to study with our group **either**.)*
2. John also likes to play tennis.
3. They also want to move to the suburbs.
4. Richard will also come.
5. He eats in that restaurant too.
6. We can also play baseball.
7. He also likes American food.
8. She is able to hear him too.
9. My parents like to listen to the radio too.
10. Mr. Johnson is also a tennis player.
11. Molly can also play this game.
12. This book was also expensive.

B. Change the following sentences from negative to affirmative.

1. Mike doesn't know her well either.
   (He also knows her well. He knows her well too.)
2. She doesn't like to watch television either.
3. Helen cannot swim well either.
4. The manager wasn't able to speak to him either.
5. They don't want to live in the suburbs either.
6. My sister won't be back before noon either.
7. He doesn't come to work by bus either.
8. Rachel isn't a friendly person either.

Any, Some

Use any *in negative sentences; use* some *in affirmative sentences.*

> Gerald took *some* books home with him.
> Gerald didn't take *any* books home with him.

A. Change the following sentences from affirmative to negative.

1. There are some extra chairs in the next room.
   *(There **aren't any** extra chairs in the next room.)*
2. We saw some good shows in New York.
3. He made some mistakes in addition.
4. They have some pretty dresses in that store.
5. The teacher taught us some important rules of addition.
6. We learned some new words in class yesterday.
7. There are some flowers in the yellow vase.
8. There are some rich men in this town.
9. We have some good neighbors.

B. Change the following sentences from negative to affirmative.

1. I didn't see any good shows on TV last night.
   *(I **saw some** good shows on TV last night.)*
2. Don't pour me any coffee.
3. We don't need any more chairs in this room.
4. There aren't any boys in the hall.
5. She doesn't want any oranges.
6. They didn't tell us about any of their experiences.
7. There aren't any good seats left for the play tonight.
8. You won't need any winter clothes in San Diego.
9. I never see any $2 bills these days.

Any, Some

C. Complete the following sentences with some *or* any.

1. I don't have _____ money with me.
   *(I don't have **any** money with me.)*
2. Please give me _____ more coffee.
3. I'm sorry, but there isn't _____ more coffee.
4. The baby is asleep. Please don't make _____ noise.
5. We need _____ oranges for breakfast.
6. I'm sorry, but I didn't have _____ time to prepare my lessons last night.
7. There aren't _____ seats available in the waiting room.
8. He never makes _____ mistakes in spelling.
9. I wanted to buy _____ fresh eggs, but there weren't _____ in the store.
10. I didn't have _____ stamps, so I went to the post office to buy _____.
11. They are having _____ trouble with the engine of their new car.
12. I never have _____ trouble with my car.
13. The teacher won't find _____ mistakes in Pat's addition.
14. She will surely find _____ in my addition.
15. I tried to borrow _____ money from him, but he said he didn't have _____.
16. She never gives the poor dog _____ water to drink.
17. Don't give _____ money to Ron. He doesn't deserve _____.
18. There aren't _____ patients in the waiting room at the moment.
19. Please put _____ water in that vase; the flowers are dying.
20. I wanted some fruit, but nobody had _____.
21. Sandy says she never has _____ fruit.
22. There are _____ famous museums in Mexico City, but we didn't have time to visit _____.
23. He never gives his patients _____ candy.
24. The doctor gave me _____ medicine for my cough.

Anyone, Someone

Use anybody, anyone, anything, *and* anywhere *in negative sentences.*

Use somebody, someone, something, *and* somewhere *in affirmative sentences.*

> We heard *someone* enter the darkened room.
> We didn't hear *anything* in the dark.

A. *Change the following sentences from affirmative to negative.*

1. He told us something about his trip.
   *(He **didn't tell** us anything about his trip.)*
2. There is someone at the door.
3. You left something on the hall table.
4. Bob will bring someone with him.
5. I lost the book somewhere downtown.
6. There is somebody in the next room.
7. Bobbie went somewhere last night with her boss.
8. He has something important to say to you.

B. *Change the following sentences from negative to affirmative.*

1. He doesn't know anything about the plan.
   *(He **knows something** about the plan.)*
2. There isn't anything the matter with Toby's ear.
3. There wasn't anyone at the door.
4. We haven't spoken to anybody about it.
5. There doesn't seem to be anybody in the office.
6. My keys aren't anywhere in this room.
7. I don't think there is anything wrong with the calculator.
8. They couldn't find her anywhere.

Possessive Pronouns

I—my—mine	we—our—ours
you—your—yours	you—your—ours
he—his—his	
she—her—hers	they—their—theirs
it—its—its	

This is *my* ring.	That is *our* truck.
This ring is *mine*.	That truck is *ours*.

A. *Substitute the appropriate possessive pronouns for the word in italics.*

1. This pen is *my pen*.
   *(This pen is **mine**.)*
2. These seats are *our seats*.
3. This umbrella is *her umbrella*.
4. These pencils are *your pencils*.
5. That computer is *my father's computer*.
6. That overcoat is *his overcoat*.
7. These magazines seem to be *your magazines;* they are not *my magazines*.
8. I believe this pen is *her pen;* it is not *my pen*.
9. Is this notebook *your notebook* or Sarah's?
10. Is this dictionary *your dictionary* or William's?
11. This pair of scissors is *her pair of scissors*.
12. These seats are *their seats;* they are not *our seats*.
13. This book is *your book;* the one over there on the desk is *my book*.
14. He drives his car to work every day and I drive *my car*.
15. You take care of your things, and I'll take care of *my things*.
16. Their home is pretty, but *our home* is prettier.
17. His pronunciation is bad, and *my pronunciation* is too.
18. His car was expensive, but *your car* was more expensive.

Possessive Pronouns

B. *In the following sentences substitute the verb* to be *for the verb* to belong. *Then introduce a possessive pronoun or the possessive form of the noun.*

1. This book *belongs* to him.
    (This book is his.)
2. This pencil *belongs* to Anthony.
    (This pencil is Anthony's.)
3. That notebook *belongs* to her.
4. That umbrella *belongs* to me.
5. I'm sure this pen *belongs* to Adrian.
6. No, it *belongs* to Miss Jefferson.
7. These magazines *belong* to them.
8. These pencils *belong* to us.
9. These books *belong* to them.
10. This book doesn't *belong* to me.
11. This pen *belongs* to him.
12. I think this desk *belongs* to Mrs. Jones.
13. That car *belongs* to Robert.
14. These green apples *belong* to us, but those yellow ones *belong* to them.
15. I think this pencil *belongs* to me, but the yellow one *belongs* to you.
16. This box of candy must *belong* to him.
17. This umbrella *belongs* to the teacher.
18. These seats *belong* to them.
19. That black sports car *belongs* to our landlord.
20. This watch doesn't *belong* to me; it *belongs* to my father.
21. The red sweater *belongs* to me; the blue one *belongs* to Virginia.
22. That bicycle *belongs* to Jim's little brother.

Possessive Pronouns

C. *Complete the following sentences with either a possessive adjective or a possessive pronoun.*

1. Jeremy lost _____ pen. Will you please lend him _____
   (*Jeremy lost **his** pen. Will you please lend him **yours?***)
2. I was on time for _____ class, but Helen was late for _____.
3. They have _____ methods of travel and we have _____.
4. We naturally prefer _____ methods, and they naturally prefer _____.
5. I found _____ notebook, but Jack couldn't find _____.
6. They think that _____ home is the prettiest on the block, and we think _____ is.
7. I left _____ pen at home. May I borrow _____ for a moment?
8. He drives to work in _____ car, and she drives to work in _____.
9. Tell William not to forget to bring _____ tennis racket, and don't forget to bring _____.
10. They swim in _____ pool and we swim in _____.
11. I have _____ vacation in June and Fern has _____ in July.
12. I found _____ umbrella, but Jill couldn't find _____.
13. We were late for _____ class, and Hope and Gwen were also late for _____.
14. Ted enjoys _____ work and I enjoy _____.
15. Each student in the school has _____ own desk and _____ own locker.
16. I borrowed money from all _____ friends, but Peg refused to borrow any money from _____.
17. We have a television set in _____ bedroom, and the boys have another set in _____.
18. Where are you going on _____ vacation? I hope to spend _____ in Europe.
19. They have _____ ideas on such matters, and we have _____.
20. We spend _____ money in one way; they spend _____ in another way.

Reflexive Pronouns

myself	ourselves
yourself	yourselves
himself	
herself	} themselves
itself	

Reflexive pronouns refer back to the subject of the sentence. The subject and object are the same person (people).

The man wounded *himself.*   The woman burned *herself.*

Supply the necessary reflexive pronouns.

1. The little girl hurt _____ when she fell.
   *(The little girl hurt **herself** when she fell.)*
2. We protect _____ from the rain with an umbrella.
3. The boy taught _____ to sew.
4. Both boys taught _____ to swim.
5. We all enjoyed _____ at the concert last night.
6. The children are amusing _____ with the kitten.
7. The policewoman shot _____ by accident.
8. Did you enjoy _____ at the party last night?
9. You will cut _____ with that knife if you are not careful.
10. I once cut _____ badly with the same knife.
11. I blame _____ for all that trouble.
12. She likes to look at _____ in the mirror.
13. My father cuts _____ every morning when he shaves.
14. Joy cut _____ on a piece of glass.
15. The child is not old enough to dress _____.
16. The dog hurt _____ when it jumped over the fence.
17. Paul and I enjoyed _____ very much at the party last night.
18. You shouldn't really blame _____ for that mistake.

Reflexive Pronouns

Reflexive pronouns are also used to give emphasis to some person or thing mentioned in the sentence.

> I *myself* will do the work.
> The car *itself* was undamaged.
> They are going to have to fix the motor *themselves*.

Supply the necessary reflexive pronouns.

1. Claude _____ will make all the preparations for the trip.
   *(Claude **himself** will make all the preparations for the trip.)*
2. I _____ will have little to do.
3. Amy said that she _____ saw the man enter the office.
4. The policeman _____ shot the thief.
5. We _____ made the first offer to buy the business.
6. The president _____ will deliver the principal address.
7. She says that she _____ will be responsible for the debt.
8. I _____ refused to take part in the matter.
9. The boys _____ will cut the grass once a week.
10. The captain _____ led the attack against the enemy.
11. The pupils _____ decorated the classroom with flags and flowers.
12. The detective _____ committed the murder.
13. I _____ don't like that restaurant.
14. It was you _____ who recommended it so highly.
15. They _____ will provide the money.
16. Jack _____ mailed the letter.
17. They _____ arranged the matter in that form.
18. You _____ must speak to him about it.
19. Janet said that she would arrange for the flowers _____.
20. I don't want to do it, but I guess I'll have to go _____.

Reflexive Pronouns

Reflexive pronouns used with by *mean alone or without help.*

She lives by *herself.*	(She lives with no other people).
He built this house by *himself.*	(No one helped him.)

In place of the word alone, *substitute the preposition* by *and the required reflexive pronoun.*

1. He went for a walk in the park alone.
    (He went for a walk in the park ***by himself.****)*
2. They made the long trip through the woods alone.
3. I don't like to go to the movies alone.
4. Kim, however, prefers to go to the movies alone.
5. Joe likes to take long walks in the woods alone.
6. The old man lives alone in a cabin in the woods.
7. Hal works alone in a small office.
8. My aunt, although she is elderly, prefers to live alone.
9. Do you like to eat alone?
10. I went to the opera last night alone.
11. The girls study alone in one group and the boys study alone in a second group.
12. One shouldn't spend too much time alone.
13. She sits alone and stares out the window all day long.
14. I can finish this work alone.
15. He prefers to do his homework alone.
16. The dog found its way home alone.
17. He plans to make a trip to Canada alone.
18. The wagon seemed to roll down the street alone.
19. We always enjoyed steering the boat alone.
20. You should try to answer the questions alone.

Present Perfect Tense

Form the present perfect tense with have (has) *and the past participle of the main verb.*

I have worked	we have worked
you have worked	you have worked
he has worked	
she has worked	} they have worked
it has worked	

The present perfect tense describes an action that happened at an indefinite time in the past.

I *have read* that book.

They *have moved* to Los Angeles.

The present perfect tense also describes an action that was repeated several times in the past.

I *have read* that book several times.

He *has studied* this lesson over and over.

Supply the present perfect tense form of the verbs in parentheses.

1. I _____. (speak) to him about it several times.
   (*I have spoken to him about it several times.*)
2. We_____ (finish) all our homework.
3. He _____ (visit) us many times.
4. She _____ (return) my book at last.
5. I am afraid that I _____ (lose) my car keys.
6. You _____ (be) in Florida many times.
7. It _____ (rain) a lot this year.
8. We _____ (learn) many new words in this course.
9. We _____ (tell) Ed what you said.
10. They _____ (hear) that story before.
11. We _____ (lend) money to them several times.
12. Mr. Katz_____ (go) to South America to work.
13. They _____ (make) that same mistake several times.
14. She _____ (see) that movie three times.
15. Harvey _____ (make) and _____ (lose) several fortunes.

* *The past participle of all regular verbs is the same as the past tense form: walked, talked, studied, etc. The past participles of irregular verbs are often very irregular and must simply be memorized. See Appendix for complete list.*

Present Perfect Tense

Present perfect tense sentences usually don't mention exact times of actions. The simple past tense is most often used to mention or imply an exact time of an action.

Past:	He *went* to Boston yesterday.
Present Perfect:	He *has gone* to Boston several times.

Past:	I *was* here last night.
Present Perfect:	I *have been* here before.

Supply either the simple past tense or the present perfect tense form as required by the meaning.

1. I _____ (go) to bed late last night; I _____ (do) this many times lately.
   *(I **went** to bed late last night; I **have done** this many times lately.)*
2. Mr. Ashe _____ (go) to Chicago last week.
3. I _____ (read) that book several times.
4. I first _____ (read) it while I was on my vacation last summer.
5. I _____ (be) in Norfolk many times.
6. Mr. Dale _____ (have) little experience in teaching that subject.
7. Billy _____ (fall) as he was crossing the street.
8. I _____ (see) Diane a few days ago.
9. When the bell rang, Wade _____ (jump) from his seat and _____ (run) from the room.
10. I _____ (try) that restaurant again and again, but I do not like the food there.
11. When I was young, I often _____ (go) fishing with my father.
12. I _____ (complete) my paper at last.
13. You _____ (start) to study English last winter.
14. The day before yesterday, we _____ (have) a bad storm.
15. I hear that you _____ (give) up the idea of studying Russian.
16. I _____ never _____ (be) to Italy.
17. It _____ (be) very cold yesterday.
18. We _____ (learn) many new words in this course.
19. The First World War _____ (begin) in 1914 and _____ (end) in 1918.
20. Rebecca says that she _____ (lose) her purse.

Present Perfect Tense

The present perfect tense also describes actions that began in the past and have continued up to the present.

> He has worked here for two years. (He is still working here.)
> They have lived here since June. (They are still living here.)

Note the difference in meaning between the following sentences:

> He has worked here for two years.   (He is still working here.)
> He worked here for two years.   (He doesn't work here anymore.)

Supply either the simple past tense or the present perfect tense form as required by the meaning.

1. I _____ (move) to Pine Street in March; I _____ (live) there for three months now.
   *(I **moved** to Pine Street in March; I **have lived** there for three months now.)*
2. We _____ (live) in Washington from 1985 to 1990.
3. Before he came to the United States, Emil _____ (work) as a carpenter.
4. Since coming here, however, he _____ (work) as a clerk.
5. My former teacher was Miss Coe. I _____ (study) with her for one year.
6. My present teacher is Mr. Ming. I _____ (study) with him for six months.
7. Juanita Chávez speaks English well because she _____ (speak) English all her life.
8. Earl _____ (work) hard all his life. (He is dead.)
9. Eric _____ (work) hard all his life. (He is alive.)
10. Ms. Pate _____ (leave) New York last month and _____ (work) in Pittsburgh since then.
11. Gail, who is now in college, _____ (study) English for ten years.
12. I myself _____ (study) English steadily since 1980.
13. Henry, who is now in the hospital, _____ (be) there for several weeks.
14. When I saw her, Linda _____ (feel) ill.
15. We _____ (buy) this car two years ago and _____ (drive) it 5,000 miles since then.
16. Up to the present time, I never _____ (be) farther west than St. Louis, Missouri.

Present Perfect Continuous Tense

Form the present perfect continuous tense with have (has) been *and the present participle of the main verb.*

I have been working   we have been working
you have been working   you have been working
he has been working
she has been working   } they have been working
it has been working

The present perfect continuous tense describes an action that began in the past and has continued up to the present. In many cases it can be used interchangeably with the present perfect tense.

They *have lived* here for five years.
They *have been living* here for five years.

Change these present perfect tense verbs from the simple to the continuous form.

1. He has worked in that firm for many years.
   (He **has been working** *in that firm for many years.*)
2. They have talked for more than an hour.
3. I have traveled all over Europe.
4. He has slept for more than ten hours.
5. It has rained all day long.
6. He has studied English for many years.
7. We have used this textbook since January.
8. She has taught science for ten years.
9. They have lived in Dallas since 1978.
10. The two nations have quarreled for many years.
11. She has taken good care of her pets.
12. They have looked everywhere for the thief.
13. He has done very little work recently.
14. Lynn has worked very hard recently.
15. You have argued about that for more than an hour.

Perfect Tenses
Negatives and Questions

Form negatives with the present perfect and present perfect continuous tenses by placing not *after* have (has). *The contractions* haven't *and* hasn't *are generally used.*

They have *not* lived there long.	They *haven't* lived there long.
It has *not* been raining.	It *hasn't* been raining.

Form questions with these perfect tenses by placing have (has) *before the subject.*

Have they lived there long?	*Has* it been raining?

A. *Change the following sentences from affirmative to negative. Use both the full form and the contracted form.*

1. You have worked very hard at your job.
   *(You **have not** worked very hard at your job. You **haven't** worked very hard at your job.)*
2. She has been teaching there many years.
3. It has been snowing.
4. I have spoken to Ms. Wolf about it.
5. You have been studying computer science.
6. He has been the best student in the class.
7. She has been taking music lessons.
8. We have been discussing the matter all day long.
9. She has been sick since Wednesday.
10. They have returned home.
11. He has known her a long time.
12. Joel has found his pen.
13. You have been absent from class all week.
14. He has told her all about it.
15. Garvin has left for San Francisco.
16. They have been having trouble with their new car.
17. He has been feeling well recently.
18. They have been married a long time.

B. *Change the sentences in Exercise A to questions.*

1. You have worked very hard at your job.
   (Have you worked very hard at your job?)

Perfect Tenses
Questions

*Change the following sentences to questions beginning with
How long.*

1. He has been working for that firm for ten years.
   (***How long*** *has he been working for that firm?*)
2. They have been married for five years.
3. They have been living in that same house for
   twenty years.
4. He has been absent from work for two weeks.
5. She has been studying computer science since June.
6. They have been arguing for more than an hour.
7. They have been friends for years.
8. He has been teaching computer science ever since he graduated from
   college.
9. It has been raining like this for an hour.
10. She has been a citizen since January.
11. He has been attending that college for four years.
12. They have occupied that same apartment for ten years.
13. He has been doing that same kind of work for many years.
14. She has been in the hospital for two months.
15. They have been driving that same car ever since I have known them.
16. The dog has been lying in that corner since this morning.
17. He has been manager of the department since February.
18. She has been waiting for him for an hour.

For, Since

For *shows the length of time of the action.*

> He has worked there *for six* months.

Since *shows the time that the action began.*

> He has worked there *since* February.

A. *Change these sentences to introduce* since *in place of* for. *Then make whatever other changes are necessary.*

1. She has been sick for three days.
   *(She has been sick **since** Wednesday.)*
2. We have been living here for three years.
3. Sue has worked for that firm for six months.
4. I have not seen him for several days.
5. I have not eaten anything for two days.
6. We have been planning this trip for a year.
7. It has been raining steadily for eight hours.
8. I have not smoked a cigarette for two years.
9. We have been waiting for you for two hours.
10. He has been in the hospital for almost a month.

B. *Change these sentences to introduce* for *instead of* since. *Then make whatever other changes are necessary.*

1. He has been absent since Monday.
   *(He has been absent **for** three days.)*
2. We haven't seen them since February.
3. We have lived in the same house since 1980.
4. They have been friends since high school.
5. It has been snowing steadily since last night.
6. They have been living with her parents since they were married.
7. He has worked for that firm since 1981.
8. I have not seen her since last week.
9. The dog hasn't eaten anything since Wednesday.
10. They haven't sent him any money since last summer.

Already, Yet

Yet *means so far; it is used in negatives and questions.*

| Sean hasn't called *yet*. | Has Sean called *yet?* |

Already *means by this time or previously; it is used in affirmative statements and questions.*

| They have *already* left. | Have they *already* left? |

A. Complete the following sentences with yet or already as required by meaning.
    1. Martha hasn't called us _____.
        *(Martha hasn't called us **yet**.)*
    2. They have _____ mailed the check.
    3. Is it time for us to leave _____? No, not _____.
    4. Sal has _____ bought the tickets for the game.
    5. We have _____ signed the contract.
    6. We have _____ been to Mexico three times.
    7. But you haven't visited Taxco _____.
    8. Has Jim gotten his new car _____?
    9. Has the meeting begun _____? No, not _____.
    10. Have the police found the thief _____?
    11. They haven't even started to look for him _____.
    12. The plane has _____ left the airport.

B. Give a negative answer with yet to the following questions.
    1. Has Mel left yet?
        *(No, Mel hasn't left **yet**.)*
    2. Has the mail arrived yet?
    3. Have you finished your homework yet?
    4. Has Mr. Dole returned from lunch yet?
    5. Have you paid that bill yet?
    6. Has the meeting begun yet?
    7. Has George found a job yet?
    8. Has the boat sailed yet?
    9. Have you bought the tickets for the game yet?
    10. Have you ridden in Pam's new car yet?

C. Give an affirmative answer with already to the questions in Exercise B.
    1. Has Mel left yet? *(Yes, Mel has **already** left.)*

Say, Tell

Use say *for direct quotations.*

> Maryanne *said,* "I am very busy."
> Yale *said* to me, "I don't feel well."

Use say *for indirect quotations when the person to whom the words are spoken is not mentioned.*

> Maryanne *said* that she was very busy.

Use tell *for indirect quotations when the person to whom the words are spoken is mentioned.*

> Bill *told* me that he didn't feel well.

Note these idiomatic uses of tell:

to tell a lie	to tell the truth	to tell time
to tell a story	to tell a secret	to tell about something

A. *Supply the correct form of* say *or* tell *in these sentences.*

1. Carol _____ that she was going to Saratoga for the weekend.
   *(Carol **said** that she was going to Saratoga for the weekend.)*
2. Carol _____ me that she was going to Saratoga for the weekend.
3. I _____ my boss (that) I could not finish my work in time.
4. Paul _____ me all about his trip. He _____ (that) it was exhausting.
5. Please_____ me about the movie which you saw last night. Ruth _____ (that) she liked it very much.
6. Grace _____ to me, "I shall never speak to him again."
7. I _____ William (that) I could not go to the movies with him.
8. The boy _____ his mother a lie, and she punished him severely. I believe he will always _____ the truth in the future.
9. The teacher _____ us (that) she was too busy to see us after class.

Say, Tell

10. These twin brothers look so much alike that I cannot _____ them apart.

11. Mr. and Mrs. Sula _____ us all about their recent trip to Japan. They _____ (that) Japan was a very interesting and picturesque country.

12. William _____ to me, "Is it necessary to write all my papers in ink?"

13. _____ me just what you _____ yesterday about your vacation plans. He _____ (that) he wanted to go with you.

14. James always _____ the truth because his parents have trained him never to _____ a lie.

15. Chan _____ (that) she was too tired to go to the park with us.

16. The teacher _____ the class (that) she was not satisfied with their work.

17. My boss _____ me (that) I could take my vacation in July.

18. Can you _____ me how I can reach Pennsylvania Station?

19. Fred _____ (that) English is difficult for him.

20. I have _____ him the same thing several times.

21. William _____ (that) the book belonged to Ms. Manley.

22. I _____ him (that) I thought it belonged to Patrick.

23. As part of his speech, the president _____ the audience several funny stories.

24. It was Kay who _____ us the secret of her success.

25. Will you please _____ me what time it is?

26. Who _____ you (that) Mr. Reese was a former army officer?

Say, Tell

B. *Change these sentences to introduce* tell *in place of* say. *Then make whatever other changes are necessary.*

1. He said that he did not feel well.
   *(He **told me** that he did not feel well.)*
2. Gene said that he could not attend the meeting.
3. She said that she had a bad headache.
4. Joseph said that he was too busy to see us.
5. George said that he didn't have enough money to buy the tickets.
6. I said that I was going to buy the tickets.
7. The student said that he didn't know the meaning of many words in the lesson.
8. The man said that there were plenty of seats available.
9. The farmer said that he expected a good crop.
10. The man said that he was German by birth.
11. He also said that he was a good friend of Lolita's.
12. Jean said that she had a lot of work to do.

C. *Change these sentences to introduce* say *instead of* tell. *Then make whatever other changes are necessary.*

1. He told us that he was too tired to go out.
   *(He **said** that he was too tired to go out.)*
2. She told us that she knew how to speak French well.
3. I told him that I was too busy to see him.
4. We told him that there were many things worse than loss of hearing.
5. The manager told us that she was not satisfied with our work.
6. The doctor told me that I must rest more.
7. He told me that he knew her well.
8. I told the children that they should not make so much noise.
9. We told them that the train was late.
10. I told him that it was useless to wait any longer.
11. He told the girls that he was not married.
12. I told the teacher that I enjoyed my lessons very much.

May

May *shows permission.*

> You *may* go in now. (You are permitted to enter.)

May *also indicates possible future action.*

> He *may* leave tomorrow. (He hasn't decided yet.)

A. *Change each of these sentences to introduce* may.

1. It is possible that he'll return later.
   *(He **may** return later.)*
2. Perhaps she'll help us with this work.
   *(She **may** help us with this work.)*
3. It is possible Len will be at the meeting tonight.
4. Perhaps Loretta will lend us the money.
5. Perhaps she will call you later.
6. Possibly Frank will offer to lend his car.
7. Possibly the weather will get warmer tomorrow.
8. It is possible that she is sick.
9. It is possible you will feel better later.
10. Perhaps it will not rain this afternoon.
11. It is possible that we shall be late for the meeting.
12. Perhaps he will not want to go with us.
13. Possibly they will go by plane.
14. Perhaps they will go to South America instead of to Europe on their vacation.

B. *Answer each of these questions using* may. *Also add* I'm not sure *at the end of your answer.*

1. Will Lois help us with the work?
   *(She **may** help us with the work. **I'm not sure**.)*
2. Will Ian pass all his examinations?
3. Will David be back by noon?
4. Will May drive us to the beach?
5. Are you going to the movies tonight?
6. Are you going to Europe on your vacation?
7. Will Nell wait for us after the lesson?
8. Will you see Liz tomorrow?
9. Will Fran lend us the money which we need?
10. Are the Kleins going to take the children with them to Toronto?

Past Perfect Tense

Form the past perfect tense with had *and the past participle of the main verb.*

I had gone	we had gone
you had gone	you had gone
he had gone	
she had gone	} they had gone
it had gone	

The past perfect tense describes an action that took place in the past before another past action. It is used in conjunction with the past tense.

By the time we arrived, they *had* already gone.
Gertrude said that she *had seen* that movie before.

Supply the past perfect tense form of the verbs in parentheses.

1. Fernando told us that he _____ (look) everywhere for the book.
   *(Fernando told us that he **had looked** everywhere for the book.)*
2. Carla _____ (leave) by the time we arrived.
3. The police reported that they finally _____ (capture) the thief.
4. I met them before I _____ (go) a hundred yards.
5. I saw that we _____ (take) the wrong road.
6. He knew that he _____ (make) a serious mistake.
7. I felt that I _____ (meet) the man somewhere before.
8. He asked me why I _____ (leave) the party so early.
9. He wanted to know what _____ (happen) to his briefcase.
10. Previously she _____ (be) a very good manager.
11. It was clear that he _____ (give) us the wrong address.
12. The teacher corrected the reports which I _____ (prepare).
13. What did he say she _____ (do) with the money?
14. He said he _____ (have) his lunch.
15. I was sure that I _____ (see) the man before.

As. . . As / So. . . As

As . . . as *expresses equality of comparison. The phrase may be used with both adverbs and adjectives. Negative constructions use* so...as.

She is as tall as he.	She is not so tall as he.
He is as old as I.	He is not so old as I.
She works as rapidly as he.	She does not work so rapidly as he.
He can run as fast as I can.	He cannot run so fast as I.

Supply the phrase as... as *or* not so...as. *Also change all adjectives to their corresponding adverb forms where necessary.*

1. Reggie is _____ (tall) _____ his brother.
   *(Reggie is **as tall as** his brother.)*

2. Our apartment is _____ (large) _____ yours.

3. This street is _____ (wide) _____ Broadway.

4. Stephen is not _____ (intelligent) _____ his sister.

5. I don't get up every morning _____ (early) _____ my parents.

6. She sings _____ (beautiful) _____ she plays.

7. We came _____ (quick) _____ we could.

8. We drove there _____ (fast) _____ we could.

9. He doesn't speak English _____ (good) _____ his sister.

10. Helen doesn't prepare her homework _____ (careful) _____ she should.

11. He doesn't attend class _____ (regular) _____ he should.

12. He didn't arrive _____ (early) _____ we expected.

13. Sharon can do the work _____ (easy) _____ I.

14. He doesn't work _____ (hard) _____ the other employees.

15. I came _____ (soon) _____ possible.

16. I don't believe that it is _____ (cold) today _____ it was yesterday.

17. Her pronunciation is not _____ (good) _____ yours.

18. We visit them _____ (often) _____ we can.

Sequence of Tenses

If the main verb of a sentence is in the past tense, all other dependent verbs are usually in the past tense too.

> He *says* he *will* bring the money tomorrow.
> He *said* he *would* bring the money tomorrow.

> I *think* I *can* come today.
> I *thought* I *could* come today.

Note the irregular past tense forms of the following auxiliaries:

will	would
can	could
may	might
have	had

A.   *Change each of the following sentences to past time.*

1. The newspaper says the President will arrive in the morning.
   *(The newspaper **said** the President **would** arrive in the morning.)*
2. She says she cannot do this work.
3. She says her name is Smith.
4. I think I can finish this report by five o'clock.
5. The meteorologist predicts that it will rain tomorrow.
6. Mr. Wick says he is very busy.
7. She complains that she has a headache.
8. He thinks he may finish his work by two o'clock.
9. I do not think I can complete this report on schedule.
10. He promises that the error will not occur again.
11. He says the mail will certainly be here by noon.
12. The students think they are making sufficient progress.
13. They say the weather will probably be cold next week.
14. I think it will rain today.
15. He hopes he can get there on time.
16. I don't think I shall see you again.
17. She says she may be late.
18. I think he is out of town.

Sequence of Tenses

19. Does she say he can't do it?
20. He complains that nobody believes a word he says.
21. I am certain that the price will go up soon.
22. She tells me that prices are sure to rise.
23. He promises faithfully that he will deliver the goods.
24. He hopes he may reach home before night.
25. He says that he has known her for many years.
26. She says she has lived here three years.
27. She thinks she can get here by noon.
28. He says he is taking English lessons from Ms. Campbell.
29. The jury declares that the prisoner isn't guilty.
30. They feel sure the battle will be over before tomorrow.
31. I wonder what changes the new chairman will introduce.
32. He swears he has never seen the man before.

B. *Change the following sentences from the past tense to the present tense.*

1. He said he would leave in the morning.
   *(He **says** he **will** leave in the morning.)*
2. They thought they had found the thief, but they were mistaken.
3. He thought the mail would surely be here by noon.
4. The paper said it would rain today.
5. She said her name was Garcia.
6. He said that he was too busy to come to class.
7. I did not think he could finish that report today.
8. He said he'd be here by noon.
9. I did not think she'd come.
10. Did he say he'd call again?
11. She promised she'd try to do better work.
12. He told me he thought prices were going up.
13. He said he had found the book.
14. She said she couldn't understand what I meant.

Have To, Must

Have to *and* must *express necessity or strong obligation.* Have to *is the more commonly used term.*

You *must* go home.	You *have to* go home.
Linda *must* work tonight.	Linda *has to* work tonight.

Substitute have to *for* must *in the following sentences.*

1. He must leave at once.
   *(He **has to** leave at once.)*
2. They must stay there at least an hour.
3. You must send it by airmail.
4. He must have more practice in conversation.
5. They must help her with that work.
6. You must speak to him about it today.
7. He must spend more time on his homework.
8. You must write them a letter.
9. We must leave before Helen gets here.
10. We must learn at least ten new words every day.
11. I must take this package to the post office.
12. You must insure it.
13. Roger must give you a receipt.
14. They must spend more time on their English.
15. You must pay more attention to pronunciation.
16. You must help her in every way possible.

Have To
Past, Future, and Present Perfect Forms

Must has no past or future tense forms. Use have to *to express obligation or necessity in the past, future, and present perfect tenses.*

> I *have to* work tonight.
> I *had to* work last night.
> I *shall have to* work tomorrow.
> I *have had to* work every night this week.

A. *Change* have to *to the past tense in these sentences.*

1. He has to get up early.
   (*He **had to** get up early.*)
2. She has to have more money.
3. Boris has to have an interpreter with him at all times.
4. Everyone has to work overtime.
5. He has to learn English quickly.
6. I have to go to the post office.
7. She has to return later.
8. He has to see the doctor a second time.
9. We have to lend him some money.
10. You have to spend more time on your homework.
11. They have to leave for New York immediately.
12. We have to stay there all summer.
13. You have to send it by air express.
14. He has to give me a receipt.

B. *Change* have to *in the sentences in Exercise A to the future tense. Add any words which may be necessary to complete the meaning.*

1. He has to get up early.
   (*He'll **have to** get up early **if he wants to be there on time.***)

Have To
Negatives and Questions

Form negatives with have to *by placing* do not, does not, did not, *or* will not *before* have. *The contracted forms* don't, doesn't, didn't, *and* won't *are generally used.*

Herb *has to* work tonight.	Herb *doesn't have to* work tonight.
She'll *have to* pay by check.	She *won't have to* pay by check.

Form questions with have to *by placing* do, does, did *or* will *before the subject.*

Herb *has to* work tonight.	*Does* Herb *have to* work tonight?
She'll *have to* pay by check.	*Will* she *have to* pay by check?

A. *Change the following sentences from affirmative to negative.*

1. The nurse had to work in the Recovery Room.
   *(The nurse **didn't** have to work in the Recovery Room.)*
2. They'll have to buy their tickets early.
3. I have to cash this check today.
4. He had to pay the doctor before leaving the office.
5. They had to go by train.
6. She has to take a make-up examination.
7. He has to write many business letters.
8. We'll have to take an earlier flight.
9. They had to wait a long time for an answer to their letter.
10. They have to learn many new words every day.
11. I have to go to the dentist again next week.
12. We had to wait in his office a long time.
13. He has to get up at six o'clock every morning.
14. They had to telephone him long distance.
15. I'll have to lend him money for the trip.
16. She has to help him with his homework every day.

B. *Change the sentences in Exercise A to questions.*

1. The nurse had to work in the Recovery Room.
   *(**Did** the nurse **have to** work in the Recovery Room?)*

Have To
Negatives and Questions

Change the following sentences to questions beginning with the question words in parentheses.

1. He had to leave at six o'clock. (What time)
   (What time did he have to leave?)
2. They had to wait there for two hours. (How long)
3. The children had to stay indoors because it was raining. (Why)
4. They had to leave the party early because Jay was sick. (Why)
5. He has to go to Denver on Sunday. (When)
6. He will have to stay there for a month. (How long)
7. They had to pay $15 for their medicine. (How much)
8. I have to go to the dentist again next week. (When)
9. You will have to come back at five o'clock. (What time)
10. He has to go to the post office to buy some stamps. (Why)
11. Each student has to learn ten new words every day. (How many new words)
12. She has to go there twice a week. (How often)
13. They had to leave twenty dollars as a deposit. (How much)
14. He has to leave at three o'clock. (What time)
15. You have to sign your name at the bottom of the page. (Where)
16. Mary has to do all the housework now because her husband is ill. (Why)
17. I'll have to ask my parents for the money. (Whom)

Preposition Review

A. *Supply the correct prepositions for these sentences.*

1. She almost got run over when she walked in front _____ a fast-moving car.
   (She almost got run over when she walked in front of a fast-moving car.)
2. The book is _____ the desk.
3. He walked _____ the room.
4. He looked _____ the window.
5. I put the letter _____ his hands.
6. The ship is now five miles _____ the port.
7. The Rocky Mountains are west _____ the Mississippi River.
8. Heat changes ice _____ water.
9. Sit _____ that chair.
10. Do you usually have dinner _____ home or _____ a restaurant?
11. He arrived _____ Hawaii _____ five o'clock.
12. Our office is six blocks _____ the station.
13. I heard it _____ the radio.
14. We stopped overnight _____ Pittsburgh.
15. Wait for us _____ the corner _____ 36th Street.
16. I'll meet you _____ front _____ the building.
17. Shelly sat here _____ me.
18. He arrived _____ five o'clock _____ a taxi.
19. The wind blew the paper_____ the window.
20. The dog jumped _____ the fence.
21. I saw him _____ the corner _____ Broadway and 42nd Street.
22. The ball rolled _____ the table _____ the floor.
23. He walked quickly _____ the door.
24. He sat down _____ the table and began to write _____ his notebook.
25. We walked _____ the street and looked _____ all the shop windows.
26. Every morning I get on the bus _____ 7:30 a.m.
27. Generally he goes _____ a walk _____ the park _____ the afternoon.
28. The thief climbed _____ the house _____ an open window.

Preposition Review

B. *Supply the correct prepositions for the following sentences.*

1. I won't be back _____ several hours. You should eat _____ me.
   (*I won't be back for several hours. You should eat **without** me.*)

2. Everyone had finished dinner _____ ten o'clock.

3. Will you lend me your pen _____ a few minutes?

4. It has been raining steadily _____ yesterday.

5. I have known Daphne _____ many years.

6. France has been a republic _____ 1871.

7. I shall wait for him _____ three o'clock.

8. The game lasted _____ three hours.

9. Yesterday I bought a new tie _____ Ivy's _____ the same time I bought a new shirt.

10. I did not finish my work _____ time to show it _____ the teacher.

11. I have been working on this _____ an hour.

12. I get up _____ seven o'clock every morning and go to bed _____ twelve.

13. I told him I would be there _____ an hour.

14. I am usually quite tired _____ the end _____ the day.

15. His health is improving day _____ day.

16. I see him _____ time _____ time.

17. Once _____ awhile I walk _____ work.

18. His office hours are _____ nine _____ five.

19. Did anyone call me _____ my absence?

20. Al arrived _____ seven o'clock sharp.

21. The train will leave _____ five minutes.

22. He didn't arrive until late _____ the afternoon.

23. I get up _____ six o'clock and have my breakfast _____ seven.

24. I have not been there _____ last summer.

25. He will be back _____ four o'clock.

26. I shall be back _____ an hour or two.

27. He has been studying English _____ two years.

Preposition Review

C. Complete the following sentences with the correct preposition.

1. I usually come to work _____ subway.
   *(I usually come to work **by subway**.)*
2. I shall do that _____ pleasure.
3. He spoke _____ a low voice.
4. The car _____ was traveling _____ full speed.
5. Shall we go _____ the bus or _____ a cab?
6. I am sorry, but I don't agree _____ you.
7. She is afraid _____ animals.
8. The messenger has just left a box of flowers _____ you.
9. He was _____ a hurry.
10. The plane flew directly _____ our house.
11. He is going to ask Grace _____ a date.
12. Some workers are paid _____ the day, others _____ the week.
13. There is something wrong _____ this telephone.
14. Please write your reports _____ ink.
15. _____ the way, have you seen Elvira lately?
16. I went there _____ mistake.
17. Bill and Gina fell _____ love _____ each other.
18. Slowly the airplane came _____ sight.
19. It is dark here. Please turn _____ the light.
20. They are both very fond _____ music.
21. There is not enough room _____ all of us.
22. I explained _____ him that the elevator was out _____ order.
23. This is an exception _____ the rule.
24. It will be impossible _____ me to go _____ you _____ the theater.
25. There is a great difference _____ that book and this one.
26. He has been absent _____ class twice this week.
27. I shall get _____ touch _____ you later this week.
28. _____ first, we sat _____ the shade _____ a large tree, but later we went _____ a swim _____ the river.

Passive Voice

The passive voice shows that the subject is receiving the action of the verb. Form the passive voice by using the appropriate form of to be *and the past participle of the main verb.*

Tense	Active Voice	Passive Voice
Present	Amy writes a letter.	A letter *is written* by Amy.
Past	Amy wrote a letter.	A letter *was written* by Amy.
Future	Amy will write a letter.	A letter *will be written* by Amy.
Present Perfect	Amy has written a letter.	A letter *has been written* by Amy.

A. *Change the following sentences from the active voice to the passive voice. Be sure to keep the same tense.*

1. Wayne delivers the mail every day.
   (The mail is delivered by Wayne every day.)
2. Fire destroyed that house.
3. The audience enjoyed the concert very much.
4. Bob took that book from the desk.
5. Walter will eat the cake.
6. Beth has finished the report.
7. Ms. Duke will leave the tickets at the box office.
8. The messenger has just left a box of flowers for you.
9. The police easily captured the thief.
10. Many people attended the lecture.
11. The movie disappointed us very much.
12. Mr. Jones manages the export division.
13. John returned the money last night.

B. *Change the following sentences from the passive voice to the active voice. Be sure to keep the same tense.*

1. That book was written by Andy Murphy.
   (Andy Murphy wrote that book.)
2. The entire city was destroyed by the fire.
3. The town was captured by the enemy.
4. The money has been stolen from my purse by someone.
5. The book was found by Mary.
6. The book has been returned by John.
7. The book is read by many people all over the world.
8. The mail is delivered by Paula.

Passive Voice

C. *Change the following sentences from active to passive. Do not change the tense.*

1. The teacher corrects our exercises at home.
    *(Our exercises **are corrected** at home **by the teacher**.)*
2. They started a dancing class last week.
3. Mr. Smith saw the accident.
4. He left the report on the desk.
5. Everybody will see this film soon.
6. He has just finished the report.
7. An economic crisis followed the war.
8. Somebody has taken my briefcase.
9. The teacher returned our written work to us.
10. Valerie buys books from that store.
11. She had finished the report by noon.
12. The mad dog bit the little boy.
13. The wind blows the fog away by midmorning.
14. The committee will choose you as its representative.
15. The maid broke the plate and the glass.
16. Tall telegraph poles lined the street.
17. The newspapers reported the event immediately.
18. We heard the sound of music.
19. The police have arrested five suspects.
20. The neighborhood children played with our dog.
21. The doctor ordered him to take a long rest.
22. Lightning struck the house.

Passive Voice

Form the passive voice of can, have to, may, must, ought to, and should with be and the past participle of the main verb.

I *have to* finish this work.	This work *has to be finished.*
You *can* see it now.	It *can be seen by* you now.
He *should* type his term paper.	His term paper *should be typed.*

Form the passive voice in the continuous tenses with being and the past participle of the main verb.

She *is lighting* the candle.	The candle *is being lighted by* her.

Change the following sentences from the active to the passive voice.

1. We may finish the leftovers in the refrigerator.
   (The leftovers in the refrigerator may be finished.)
2. They should send it to us at once.
3. The mailman is delivering the mail now.
4. He has to finish it today.
5. The police are holding him for further questioning.
6. They may organize a new group next week.
7. You ought to send the package by registered mail.
8. The citizens are defending the city bravely.
9. They cannot hold the meeting in that room.
10. They may deliver the merchandise while we are out.
11. He has to pay the bill before the first of the month.
12. He may pay the bill for us.
13. Congress is debating that question today.
14. For the time being, Karen is teaching that group.
15. You ought to water the plant once a week.
16. The company is shipping the merchandise today.
17. We must warn them of the danger.
18. They couldn't sell the house at that price.
19. They are sending my aunt to Europe on a special mission.
20. You should insure the package.

Passive Voice

Negatives and Questions

Form negatives in the passive voice by placing not *after the auxiliary verb. The contracted forms are often used.*

> The film *was not directed* by Steven Spielberg.
> The bricks *won't be delivered* before Tuesday.

Form questions in the passive voice by placing the auxiliary verb before the subject.

> *Was* the film *directed* by Steven Spielberg?
> *Will* the bricks *be delivered* before Tuesday?

A. *Change the following sentences from affirmative to negative. Use the full form and the contracted form.*

1. He was sent to Los Angeles.
2. This must be finished today.
3. The letter has already been sent.
4. The book was published in 1982.
5. The class is taught by Ms. Smith.
6. The merchandise is being sent today.
7. The thief has been caught by the police.
8. The fire was started by an arsonist.
9. The chairs have been put in Room 10.
10. The jewels were stolen by one of the servants.
11. The book will be published in the spring.
12. The lecture was attended by many people.
13. The first prize was won by Maria.
14. The accident was caused by Vance's carelessness.
15. Our exercises will be corrected each night.
16. The house was completely destroyed by the fire.
17. The tickets have been purchased.
18. The bridge was designed by a French architect.
19. The contract will be signed tomorrow.
20. The packages are delivered daily.
21. The cries of the child were heard by everyone.
22. The house was struck by lightning.

B. *Change the sentences in Exercise A to questions.*

1. He was sent to Los Angeles.
   (Was he sent to Los Angeles?)

Passive Voice
Questions

C. *Change the following sentences to questions beginning with the question word in parentheses.*

1. The house was built in 1975. (When)
   *(**When** was the house built?)*
2. The building was destroyed by fire. (How)
3. The merchandise will be delivered next week. (When)
4. The money had been stolen by the workers. (By whom)
5. The child was finally found in the park. (Where)
6. He was injured in an airplane accident. (In what kind of accident)
7. The mail is delivered at ten o'clock. (What time)
8. The contract must be signed by Mr. Smith. (When)
9. The tickets will be left at the box office. (Where)
10. San Francisco was nearly destroyed by earthquake in 1906. (In what year)
11. The book was published in France. (Where)
12. He was operated on for appendicitis. (What)
13. The boy was punished because he had run away. (Why)
14. The note was left on the table. (Where)
15. The city was captured by the enemy in June. (In what month)
16. The money was put into the safe. (Where)
17. The bridge will be finished this year. (When)
18. It was designed by a French engineer. (Who)

Supposed To

Supposed to *used with the simple form of the main verb expresses anticipation or expectation. This term has a present and a past tense.*

> Ms. Garcia *is supposed to* be here. (Present)
> We *were supposed to* arrive last night, but we were delayed. (Past)

Supply the correct form of to be supposed to.

1. Doris and I _____ (send) the plans last night.
   *(Doris and I **were supposed to send** the plans last night.)*
2. The ship _____ (sail) at two o'clock this afternoon.
3. She _____ (come) at four o'clock yesterday afternoon.
4. He _____ (be) here now.
5. Lilly _____ (bring) the books with her.
6. That letter _____ (write) yesterday.
7. I _____ (mail) this package last Saturday.
8. He _____ (leave) for Europe next week, but he may have to postpone his trip until next month.
9. He _____ (take) his lesson at ten o'clock, but we haven't seen him.
10. In which room is the club _____ (meet)?
11. The bridge club _____ (meet) in Room 10, but the other club _____ (meet) on the tenth floor.
12. On which line am I _____ (write) my name?
13. I'm sorry that I must leave so soon, but I _____ (be) at the consulate at twelve o'clock.
14. Ann wants to know whether she _____ (take) her pill at ten o'clock or twelve o'clock.
15. The catalogue _____ (publish) next spring.

Used To

Used to *describes an action that was customary or that happened for some time in the past but that does not happen at the present time.*

> We lived in Maryland before we moved here.
> We *used to* live in Maryland.

> I taught English for years; now I'm retired.
> I *used to* teach English.

In each of the following sentences, change the italicized verb to introduce used to.

1. I *walked* to work.
   (**I used to walk** to work.)
2. I never *made* so many mistakes in spelling.
3. The accounting department *was* on the 18th floor.
4. Tom *was* a good employee and *worked* hard.
5. I *bought* all my clothes in that store.
6. This building *was* occupied by a large insurance firm.
7. Betty *had* charge of the transportation division.
8. Gary *played* the violin.
9. Laura *went* to the concert every week.
10. He never *did* his work poorly.
11. He *took* a great interest in his piano lessons.
12. All meetings *were* held in the auditorium.
13. Marcus *was* the official interpreter for the company.
14. I *used* my computer a great deal.
15. Mr. Earl *worked* in this office.
16. I never *caught* cold.
17. It *was* my custom to practice the piano every day.

Would Rather

Would rather *followed by the simple form of the verb means to* prefer. *The contracted form* 'd rather *is generally used. Note the position and use of* than.

> I would *rather* watch TV *than* go to a movie.
> She'd *rather* walk *than* take a taxi.
> We'd *rather* go to the cabin this weekend. (an implied comparison with any other choice)

Change these sentences to introduce would rather. *Use both the full form and the contracted form. Be sure that* rather *appears only once in each clause.*

1. I prefer to wait outside rather than in here.
   (*I **would rather** wait outside than in here. I'd **rather** wait outside than in here.*)
2. They prefer to walk to school.
3. We prefer to spend the summer at home instead of in the country.
4. The doctor says that he prefers to examine you in his office.
5. I prefer not to mention it to him at this time.
6. I prefer to eat at home rather than in a restaurant.
7. He prefers to meet us downtown.
8. I prefer to speak with her in private.
9. I prefer to drive a small car rather than a big one.
10. Jean prefers to study in this class instead of in the advanced class.
11. I prefer to do all my homework before I leave school.
12. He prefers to live in a large city like London.
13. I prefer to live in a small town.
14. I prefer to work in my garden rather than play golf.
15. I prefer to see a good movie rather than go to the opera.
16. He prefers to attend a large college; I prefer to go to a small one.

Had Better

Had better *with the simple form of the verb means* it would be better *or* it would be advisable. *The contracted form* 'd better *is generally used . Note that this term expresses a future thought even though it is in a past form.*

You *had better* see a doctor.   You *'d better* see a doctor.

Change these sentences to introduce had better. *Use the full form and the contracted form.*

1. It would be better if you came back later.
   *(You **had better** come back later. You'd **better** come back later.)*
2. It would be better if she rested a while.
3. It would be better if Betty gave you back the money.
4. It would be better if she didn't see him again.
5. It would be advisable for them to save their money.
6. It would be better if you didn't mention this to anyone.
7. It would be advisable for you to send an invitation.
8. It would be better if you didn't tell Carmen about this.
9. It would be advisable for you to tell them the truth.
10. It would be better if Neil prepared his homework more carefully.
11. It would be advisable for you not to drive so fast on this road.
12. You shouldn't give them too much information.
13. You should notify the police at once.
14. I advise you to spend more time on your piano lessons.

Tag Endings

Tag endings ask a question or invite confirmation of some fact we already know. Tag endings contain a pronoun and an auxiliary verb but not a main verb. Use a negative tag ending after an affirmative sentence.

> Cyril can speak English, *can't he?*
> She's an American, *isn't she?*
> You live in Virginia, *don't you?*
> They'll be at the party, *won't they?*

Add the correct tag ending to the following sentences.

1. She goes shopping every day, _____?
   *(She goes shopping every day, **doesn't she?**)*
2. He has been studying English a long time, _____?
3. Matthew is a good student, _____?
4. She plays the piano well, _____?
5. She can play the piano well, _____?
6. You played tennis yesterday, _____?
7. The traffic is heavy today, _____?
8. It was also heavy yesterday, _____?
9. You always buy your clothes at a department store, _____?
10. They go for a walk in the park every Sunday, _____?
11. You'll be back before noon, _____?
12. You have read that book, _____?
13. They are very old friends, _____?
14. It takes more than an hour to get there, _____?
15. The bus stops at this corner, _____?
16. They are traveling in Europe now, _____?
17. I gave you what you wanted, _____?
18. She was unkind to you, _____?
19. You could drive that truck, _____?

Tag Endings

Use an affirmative tag ending after a negative sentence.

> Carl can't speak English, *can he?*
> She isn't an American, *is she?*
> You don't live in Virginia, *do you?*
> They won't be at the party, *will they?*

A. Add the correct tag ending to the following sentences.

1. Catherine doesn't like to study geometry, _____ ?
    *(Catherine doesn't like to study geometry, **does she?**)*

2. You haven't ever been in South America, _____?

3. You won't mention this to anyone, _____?

4. The traffic today isn't very heavy, _____?

5. It wasn't heavy yesterday either, _____?

6. They didn't go by plane, _____?

7. Beth didn't say anything to you about it, _____?

8. He wasn't driving fast at the time, _____?

9. She doesn't know how to dance, _____?

10. Joe won't be back before noon, _____?

11. The bus doesn't stop near here, _____?

12. You didn't write those letters, _____?

13. I haven't paid you yet, _____?

14. Helen isn't going with you, _____?

15. You haven't had your lunch yet, _____?

16. He can't speak English, _____?

17. I shouldn't drive so fast on this road, _____?

18. We won't have enough money to get in, _____?

19. They wouldn't give you the information, _____?

Tag Endings

B. *Add the correct tag endings to these sentences.*

1. Gregory left class early today, _____?
    *(Gregory left class early today, **didn't he?**)*
2. He is an excellent student, _____?
3. She has never gotten in touch with you, _____?
4. Today is Wednesday, _____?
5. You live in Minnesota, _____?
6. You were absent yesterday, _____?
7. Both men look very much alike, _____?
8. They don't know each other, _____?
9. This street runs north and south, _____?
10. We won't have to stand in line, _____?
11. You mailed that letter, _____?
12. You didn't forget to put a stamp on it, _____?
13. She can speak French well, _____?
14. He never comes to class on time, _____?
15. The train is supposed to arrive soon, _____?
16. This bus stops at the airport, _____?
17. She is making good progress in French, _____?
18. Your sister has been sick a long time, _____?
19. This is your umbrella, _____?
20. There is someone at the door, _____?
21. The telephone rang, _____?
22. They paid you what they owed you, _____?
23. You'll call me in the morning, _____?
24. It hasn't come true yet, _____?
25. My mother has spoken to you, _____?

Tag Endings

C. *Add tag endings to the following sentences.*

1. He speaks English well, _____?
    *(He speaks English well, **doesn't he?**)*

2. She writes a lot of letters, _____?

3. He is a busy man, _____?

4. He makes a lot of mistakes in pronunciation, _____?

5. Gail spends a lot of money on clothes, _____?

6. He always comes to class on time, _____?

7. Tony is out of town, _____?

8. There are a lot of students absent from class, _____?

9. They are good friends, _____?

10. They watch television every night, _____?

11. You enjoy your computer science class, _____?

12. The mail is delivered at ten o'clock, _____?

13. You spend a lot of time with them, _____?

14. She has to work very hard, _____?

15. He is too old to play football, _____?

16. You have piano lessons twice a week, _____?

17. The plane arrives at noon, _____?

18. They visit you every Sunday, _____?

19. You get up early every morning, _____?

20. He sits in the front row, _____?

21. She works in the import department, _____?

22. He is a good salesman, _____?

D. *Change the sentences in Exercise C to the past and add the tag endings.*

1. He speaks English well, _____?
    *(He spoke English well, **didn't he?**)*

E. *Change the sentences in Exercise C to the future with will and add the tag endings.*

1. He speaks English well, _____?
    *(He'll speak English well, **won't he?**)*

115

It, There

The impersonal pronoun it *is used in expressions of weather, time, and distance.*

> *It* is cold today.   *It* is ten o'clock.
>
> *It* is a long way from here to California.

It *is also used with the verb* to be, *an adjective, and an infinitive.*

> *It is easy to learn* English grammar.
>
> *It was difficult to find* your address.

When it *or* there *is used to express the existence of an object or objects, some other word in the sentence is the subject.*

> *There* is a fly in the room. (*Fly* is the subject.)
>
> *It* was I who called you yesterday. (*I* is the subject.)
>
> *There* are twelve people on that jury. (*People* is the subject.)

A. Complete the following sentences with It is *or* There is.

1. _____ raining very hard.
   (It is raining very hard.)
2. _____ plenty of time to do that later.
3. _____ a strange man in Bertha's office.
4. _____ easy to understand why he is angry.
5. _____ time for you to take your medicine.
6. _____ almost ten o'clock.
7. _____ a new moon tonight.
8. _____ a cat in one of your flower beds.
9. _____ impossible to finish that work in such a short time.
10. _____ warm in this room.
11. _____ beginning to rain.
12. _____ ten miles from here to the university.
13. _____ a mailbox on the corner.
14. _____ a long line of cars ahead of us.
15. _____ a pity that he must stop his English class.
16. _____ a lot of static on our radio.
17. _____ easy to understand her accent.

It, There

B. *Complete the following sentences with* It *or* There.

1. _____ is raining very hard.
   *(**It** is raining very hard.)*
2. _____ is a letter for you on the hall table.
3. _____ is almost three o'clock.
4. _____ is a very nice day.
5. _____ are several Germans in our English class.
6. _____ is very hot in this room.
7. _____ is difficult to speak English well.
8. _____ is not a cloud in the sky.
9. _____ is beginning to snow.
10. _____ is hard to learn English in such a short time.
11. _____ are a lot of beautiful homes on this street.
12. _____ is a shame that you can't come with us.
13. _____ was Peg who told me about the changes.
14. _____ is no place like home.
15. _____ is a pity she can't speak English.
16. _____ is a long way from here to Honolulu.
17. _____ are a lot of people in the park this afternoon.
18. _____ was almost eight o'clock when they arrived.
19. _____ were a lot of employees absent today.
20. _____ is Tuesday, isn't it?
21. _____ is someone at the door, isn't there?
22. _____ is very unpleasant to work in this cold room.
23. _____ is dangerous to drive so fast.
24. _____ are only twenty-eight days in February.

It, There

C. *Change the following sentences so that each one begins with* It.

1. Learning English is not easy.
   (***It** is not easy to learn English.*)
2. Learning new words every day is important.
3. Studying with Mr. Nathan is very rewarding.
4. To pay so much money for a car that is old is foolish.
5. To drive so fast is dangerous.
6. Traveling in foreign countries is interesting.
7. To be able to speak a foreign language is often helpful.
8. To blame Rocky for that mistake is unfair.
9. Studying grammar is not interesting for a lot of students.
10. Understanding grammar is important.
11. Getting up early in the morning is almost impossible for me.
12. Going by bus is faster than going by car.
13. To sing in such a low key is not easy for a soprano.
14. To explain this matter to him will be difficult.
15. Working twelve hours a day at your age is foolish.
16. Spending the afternoon at the beach will be pleasant.
17. To call her at this late hour would be unwise.
18. Eating quickly is not satisfying.
19. Accepting their apologies is not easy.
20. Being comfortable in such hot weather is demanding.
21. Competing for the top prize is their main goal.

It, There

D. *Change the following sentences by beginning each one with*
   There is *or* There are.

1. A new magazine is on the hall table.
   (*There is* *a new magazine on the hall table.*)
2. A lot of trees are in the park.
3. Two strange men are in the living room.
4. Several people are waiting to see Dr. Quarles.
5. A letter for you is in the mailbox.
6. A storm is approaching.
7. A lot of dark clouds are in the sky.
8. Two policemen are on the corner.
9. A dog is in the garden.
10. Two children are playing on your front lawn.
11. Only one window is in the room.
12. Two tall trees are in front of the house.
13. A blackboard is in every room.
14. Several pictures are on the wall of each room.
15. A lot of birds of various colors are in the trees.
16. A vase of flowers is on the table.
17. An inch of snow is on the ground.
18. Curtains are on each window.
19. A lot of Swedes are in my English class.
20. A mailbox is on the corner.
21. The report is on his desk.
22. Two tickets to the new show are waiting for you at the box office.
23. Some contracts are in his briefcase.

Gerunds

A gerund is a form of verb that functions as a noun and ends in ing. Certain verbs, like enjoy, mind, stop, consider, appreciate, *and* finish, *can be followed by gerunds but not infinitives.*

He *enjoys studying* English.
I *finished reading* the lesson.
He *has stopped trying* to be first.

In the sentences below, supply the gerund form of the verb shown in parentheses.

1. I am considering _____ (move) back to Montreal.
   *(I am considering **moving** back to Montreal.)*
2. I enjoy _____ (study) with Ms. Kinsey.
3. Mr. Kent stopped _____ (go) to his English class.
4. Do you mind _____ (wait) a few minutes in the hall?
5. We are considering _____ (buy) a compact disc player.
6. Did you enjoy _____ (travel) through Canada last summer?
7. Ask that salesman whether he minds _____ (come) back this afternoon.
8. Mr. Lamb enjoys _____ (listen) to the radio.
9. Mr. and Mrs. Michaels have stopped _____ (use) their camcorder.
10. They resent _____ (hold) the classes in the evening instead of the morning.
11. We shall avoid_____ (receive) visitors after 2:00 p.m.
12. They have finished _____ (paint) our apartment at last.
13. Paul was driving fast and couldn't avoid _____ (hit) the other car.
14. Joey denied _____ (take) the book.
15. You shouldn't risk _____ (go) out if you have a cold.
16. He admitted _____ (make) the mistake after we questioned him for a long time.

Gerunds

Gerunds may also be used after most prepositions but not after to *when it is part of an infinitive.*

> Jane is fond of *exercising*.
> We use this pot for *brewing* herb tea.

Gerunds are used after the expressions to be worth, no use, *and* do you mind.

> The new Lucas film *is worth seeing*.
> It's *no use trying* to call them at this hour.
> *Do you mind riding* for an hour to work?

A. Supply the gerund of the verb in parentheses. Where necessary, introduce a preposition.

1. Were you successful _____ (see) Ms. Vaughn?
   (Were you successful in seeing Ms. Vaughn?)
2. Is Kay fond _____ (swim)?
3. He needs much more drill _____ (spell).
4. There's no use _____ (call) Mr. Dennis. He's not at home now.
5. There is little chance _____ (see) him today.
6. That salesman has left. He got tired _____ (wait) for Ms. Moreno.
7. That book is well worth _____ (read).
8. Do you mind _____ (live) in the city?
9. It is a question _____ (find) the right person for the job.
10. Mr. Spock always takes great pleasure _____ (help) others.
11. Do you think that lecture is worth _____ (attend)?
12. Mr. and Mrs. Johnson are thinking _____ (move) to Colorado.
13. He insisted _____ (help) me with the report.
14. Would you mind _____ (hold) this for me, please.
15. Mr. Peters spoke this morning _____ (start) a new class.
16. He has no intention _____ (leave) the class at this time.
17. We are all looking forward _____ (see) Ms. Robertson next week.
18. Is there any possibility _____ (see) Mr. Black this morning?

Gerunds

B. *Using a gerund construction, complete the following sentences in your own words.*

1. She is not interested in _____ .
   *(She is not interested in **learning to speak English**.)*
2. We both enjoy _____ .
3. We went straight home instead of _____ .
4. I don't feel like _____ .
5. He has no intention of _____ .
6. Do you think that book is worth _____ ?
7. We congratulated him on _____ .
8. Do you mind _____ ?
9. He is tired of _____ .
10. He left suddenly without _____ .
11. Thank you for _____ .
12. He insisted upon _____ .
13. I can't imagine _____ .
14. We are considering _____ .
15. He says he doesn't feel like _____ .
16. They have stopped _____ .
17. There is little chance of _____ .
18. He hasn't had any experience in _____ .
19. You can't blame him for _____ .
20. We all need more practice in _____ .
21. We finally succeeded in _____ .
22. They are thinking of _____ .
23. They are both very fond of _____ .
24. In the middle of our discussion, the man suddenly burst out _____ .
25. Have you finished _____ ?
26. Mrs. Belkamp has suggested _____ .
27. If we don't hurry, we'll miss _____ .
28. The Cresseys had to postpone _____ .
29. Did the prisoner escape _____ ?
30. Would you mind _____ ?

Gerunds and Infinitives

Certain verbs can be followed by either gerunds or infinitives. Some of these verbs are start, begin, continue, like, neglect, hate, cease, love, prefer, and intend.

> He has *begun to take* English lessons.
> He has *begun taking* English lessons.

> She will *continue to study* in that class.
> She will *continue studying* in that class.

A. Complete each of the following sentences with a gerund.

1. Micky intends _____ (take) biology this semester.
   *(Micky intends **taking** biology this semester.)*
2. He likes _____ (take) lessons from Miss Dixson.
3. I neglected _____ (tell) Mr. Hall about that report.
4. They prefer _____ (meet) at five o'clock instead of at six.
5. Joe will start _____ (work) in that department next week.
6. But he will continue _____ (take) frequent trips to the Midwest.
7. Meg loves _____ (work) for Mr. Harris.
8. He intends _____ (leave) on the fifteenth.
9. He hates _____ (leave) the East Coast.
10. When will Mr. Hale start _____ (come) to class?
11. Ava likes _____ (study) in the fourth grade.
12. Mr. Hope prefers _____ (take) private lessons.
13. We hope to begin _____ (increase) our sales in the spring.
14. The enemies have continued _____ (build) up their armies.
15. Mary hates _____ (do) secretarial work.

B. Complete each of the sentences in Exercise A with an infinitive.

1. Micky intends _____ (take) biology this semester.
   *(Micky intends **to take** biology this semester.)*

Future Perfect Tense

Form the future perfect tense with will have *and the past participle of the main verb. The contracted form* 'll *is often used.*

I shall have worked	we shall have worked
you will have worked	you will have worked
he will have worked	
she will have worked	} they will have worked
it will have worked	

The future perfect tense describes an action that will be a past and complete action at a certain point in the future.

By next September I *'ll* have worked here thirty years.
We shall *have finished* this book in June.

Complete the following sentences with the future perfect tense form of the verbs in parentheses.

1. I am sure they _____ (complete) the new road by June.
   (I am sure they'll have completed the new road by June.)
2. He says that before he leaves he _____ (see) every show in town.
3. If you don't make a note of that appointment, you _____ (forget) it by next week.
4. By this time next month, all the roses _____ (die).
5. By January first, all our work for the year _____ been _____ (finish) and our report _____ been _____ (turn) in.
6. By the time you arrive, I _____ (finish) reading your book.
7. I _____ (be) in this country two years on January 12.
8. By this time next year, you _____ (forget) all your present troubles.
9. A century from now, wars, I hope, _____ (become) a thing of the past.
10. Perhaps by that time, we _____ (learn) that it is better to cooperate than to fight.
11. If he hasn't begun to study yet, he certainly _____ not _____ (learn) all his lessons by tomorrow.
12. I hope that by this time next year a peace treaty _____ been _____ (sign).
13. When you are my age, you _____ (learn) much.
14. A year from now he _____ (take) his medical exams and begun to practice.

Review of Verb Tenses

A. *Complete the following sentences with the correct tense of the verbs in parentheses.*

1. Daryl always _____ (come) to work on time.
   *(Daryl always **comes** to work on time.)*

2. Mr. Jones _____ (teach) us at present. He _____ (substitute) for Mr. Holt, who is our regular teacher.

3. I _____ (work) in my garden when you called me last night.

4. We _____ (take) our finals next week.

5. I _____ (come) to work on the bus this morning.

6. As I _____ (come) to work this morning, I _____ (meet) a boy who tried _____ (sell) me a watch.

7. I _____ (be) to the Grand Canyon several times.

8. Listen! I think the telephone _____ (ring).

9. Bob said that he _____ (see) that movie before.

10. I _____ (read) that novel three or four times.

11. By this time next year, we _____ (complete) all the exercises in this book.

12. Your telegram _____ (come) just as I _____ (leave) my house.

13. The sun _____ (shine) brightly when I got up this morning.

14. Our class _____ (begin) every morning at 8:30 and _____ (end) at 10:00.

15. We occasionally _____ (go) to the movies on Sunday.

16. Listen! Somebody _____ (knock) at the door.

17. Up to now, nothing _____ (hear) from the search party.

18. Marjory, who is now in the fourth grade, _____ (study) English for three years.

19. Ruth _____ (study) French for a few months last year.

20. My brother-in-law _____ (come) to visit me next week.

Review of Verb Tenses

B. *Complete these sentences with the correct tense of the verbs in parentheses.*

1. The magician _____ (do) tricks on the stage when we entered.
   *(The magician **was doing** tricks on the stage when we entered.)*

2. The newspaper says that the police in New Orleans finally _____ (catch) the bank robber.

3. Look! _____ (be) that Colonel Evans _____ (cross) the street?

4. _____ she usually _____ (walk) along Spencer Street at the same time every morning?

5. She said that she _____ (leave) before she heard the news.

6. By this time next week, Rod and Alan _____ (visit) their grandmother.

7. By March fifteenth, I _____ (be) here one year.

8. Deborah handed in the report which she _____ (write).

9. Lee usually _____ (study) very hard. In fact, whenever I _____ (see) him he _____ (study) something.

10. Have you any idea what she _____ (do) when I _____ (call) her tomorrow?

11. What _____ you _____ (do) when I called you last night?

12. Since when _____ Harry _____ (be) manager of this department?

13. He _____ (be) appointed last June and _____ (be) in charge ever since.

14. Where _____ (be) you _____ (go) on your vacation next month?

15. He cooked the rabbit which he _____ (shoot) previously in the woods.

16. The sun _____ (shine) when I got up this morning, but by ten o'clock it _____ (disappear) behind the clouds.

17. The U.S. Civil War _____ (begin) in 1861 and it _____ (end) in 1865, but not before many thousands of men _____ (meet) their deaths.

18. Is there any possibility _____ (see) Mr. Black this morning?

Review of Verb Tenses

C. *Complete these sentences with the correct tense of the verbs in parentheses.*

1. Tod _____ (feel) refreshed by the lemonade he _____ (drink) with us earlier.
    *(Tod obviously **felt** refreshed by the lemonade he **had drunk** with us earlier.)*

2. Friends who _____ (tell) us the truth are often less appreciated than those who _____ (flatter) us.

3. What did you do when you discovered that you _____ (lose) your wallet?

4. While we _____ (drive) to Milwaukee, we _____ (have) two flat tires.

5. The minute the bell rang, the students _____ (jump) from their seats.

6. When we got home from work, we discovered that they _____ (come) and _____ (go.)

7. Ms. Sheldon _____ (trip) as she _____ (enter) the room.

8. Sidney _____ (choose) captain of the baseball team by the other players.

9. That movie _____ (see) by millions of people around the world.

10. Lilian noticed that we _____ (take) the wrong road.

11. My mother can't _____ (see) well after dark, so she doesn't _____ (drive) at night.

12. She hasn't been able to start _____ (dance) again because her broken leg _____ (heal) yet.

13. I intend _____ (go) to Greece on my vacation.

14. Where _____ you _____ (go) on your last vacation?

15. Where _____ you _____ (go) on your next vacation?

16. Where _____ you usually _____ (go) on your vacations?

17. What _____ you _____ (do) right now?

Position of Adverbs

Place adverbs of time (yesterday, last week, next month, etc.) at the beginning or end of a sentence.

> I saw Ms. Anderson *yesterday.*
> *On Wednesday* you are due in court.

Place adverbs of frequency (often, usually, generally, rarely, ever, etc.) before the main verb except when the main verb is a form of to be.

> He *always* comes to class late.   She is *never* late for class .
> Does he *always* come to class late?   Is she *always* late for class?

Note that in sentences with auxiliary verbs, adverbs of frequency are after the auxiliary verbs but before the main verbs.

> He has *always* come late to class.
> We don't *usually* eat in the cafeteria.

Place the indicated adverb in the correct place in these sentences.

1. I saw Mr. Manchester in the cafeteria. (yesterday)
   *(I saw Mr. Manchester in the cafeteria **yesterday**.)*
2. Sam has been a very careful worker. (always)
3. He goes to Boston on business trips. (often)
4. He stays with me. (seldom)
5. She accepted the raise. (cheerfully)
6. She plays the piano. (well)
7. He is planning to visit us at our home. (tonight)
8. She has spoken to me. (never)
9. Alice replaced the pieces. (carefully)
10. Al is late for class. (always)
11. He has prepared his lessons. (always)
12. We went for a walk in the park. (on Sunday)

Position of Adverbs

13. We go for a walk in the park on Sunday. (usually)
14. Do you go for a walk on Sunday? (ever)
15. I go for a walk on Sunday. (never)
16. I spoke to Ellen about that matter. (on Tuesday)
17. He promised to give me an answer. (in the morning)
18. Have you visited Chicago? (ever)
19. Do you eat in the cafeteria? (usually)
20. Have you eaten in the cafeteria? (ever)
21. Have you finished writing your exercises? (yet)
22. I have spoken to him about that. (often)
23. Have you spoken to him about that? (ever)
24. Has he been late for his classes? (always)
25. I have been to Mt. Vernon, Washington's home. (never)
26. I have read that book. (twice)
27. I have read it. (never) Have you read it? (ever)
28. Mr. and Mrs. Smith visited their daughter in college. (last week)
29. He is too busy to eat lunch. (often)
30. He is leaving for Denver. (tomorrow)
31. Does she forget her key? (sometimes)
32. Does she get up early? (generally)
33. Has he been taller than his sister? (always)
34. Nobody has a bad word to say about Kay. (ever)
35. He always does his work. (cheerfully)
36. He does his exercises. (rarely) (carefully)
37. Belinda is going to leave for California. (tomorrow)
38. I met him there. (yesterday)

Word Order

Word order is very important in English sentences. The normal word order for an English statement is subject, verb, indirect object, direct object, adverbial modifiers. Be careful not to separate a verb and its direct object with an adverbial modifier.

| Wrong: | I saw *yesterday* my friend. |
| Correct: | I saw my friend *yesterday*. |

Reconstruct the following sentences and put them into good English form.

1. Jacob has been two years in this country.
   (Jacob has been in this country two years.)
2. He is studying now engineering at Columbia University.
3. He was so excited he hardly could think.
4. The light was so bright that we had to cover from time to time our eyes.
5. She said that he had had already three operations.
6. I even didn't know that it was you who was calling me.
7. Throw me from the bus a kiss.
8. Karen went to see the mayor in a new skirt.
9. Louise comes sometimes to our house for the lesson, and I go sometimes to hers.
10. I used to like a lot the theater, but now I go every night to the movies.
11. Of course, always I speak German with my family and friends.
12. He is studying now French as well as English.
13. He has been two years here; perhaps it is more even than that.
14. It was so cold that summer that we had to wear now and then our overcoats.
15. I have every day to write a lot of letters in English.
16. He said that he had seen already that movie.
17. He comes seldom to the lesson on time.
18. Simon gave me this morning your message.
19. Please read slowly the whole sentence.
20. We went last night to the theater.

Still, Anymore

Still *means* even up to the present time. *It indicates some continuing action.* Still *usually comes before the main verb.*

> He is *still* working in that office.   They *still* live in that house.

Anymore *indicates that an action that went on in the past has been discontinued. We usually place* anymore *at the end of a negative sentence.*

> He isn't working in that office *anymore.*
> They don't live in that house *anymore.*

A. *Complete the following sentences with* still *or* anymore.

1. He doesn't study in this class.
    *(He doesn't study in this class **anymore.**)*
2. She is _____ working as a clerk in a department store.
3. He is _____ teaching geography in that same school.
4. Sue is _____ the best student in the class.
5. Ann is not the best student in the class _____.
6. We never see you at the school dances _____.
7. They don't live near us _____.
8. I seldom see George _____.
9. We are _____ good friends, although I rarely see them.
10. Do they _____ spend each summer in Mexico City?
11. He _____ thinks that he is the best teacher in the department.
12. Dr. Jones is not our doctor _____.
13. I _____ think that Helen is the most interesting person in the whole school.
14. They are _____ bitter enemies, although they never see each other

B. *Change the following sentences from affirmative to negative.*

1. We are still good friends.
    *(We are not good friends **anymore.**)*
2. He is still president of the club.
3. They still live on State Street.
4. They still visit each other regularly.
5. He is still in love with her.
6. They are still living in Quito.
7. We still see them at the club on Saturday night.
8. It is still raining.

Direct and Indirect Speech

A direct quotation gives the words of a speaker exactly as spoken.

Tammy said, "I am leaving tomorrow."

An indirect quotation reports on someone's words indirectly. The pronouns used in an indirect quotation are different from those in a direct quotation. (Review page 94 for sequence of tenses using to say.)

Tammy said that she was leaving tomorrow.

When an indirect object (page 34) is used in a sentence being changed from direct to indirect speech, say to *is often changed to* tell.

Direct: Barbara *said* to Phyllis, "I have a cold."
Indirect: Barbara *told* Phyllis that she had a cold.

Change the following sentences from direct to indirect speech.

1. Carolyn said, "I shall be here at noon."
   (Carolyn said she would be here at noon.)
2. David said, "The plane will probably get in late."
3. The boss said, "I have to finish this report by tonight."
4. The doctor said, "She'll get well quickly."
5. The teacher said, "Everyone has to write a three-page paper for tomorrow."
6. Richard said, "I saw that movie last week."
7. Janie said, "I've read that book."
8. Suzanne said to her boyfriend, "I can't go tonight."
9. William said to me, "I'll finish this tomorrow."
10. She said to him, "The lights aren't working."
11. I said to the waitress, "This bill is wrong."
12. The boy said, "I'm only eight years old."
13. Henry said, "I can meet them later."
14. Ms. Bremer said, "I don't do business that way."

Indirect Speech
Questions

Questions in indirect speech are expressed as statements.

> Direct: Peter asked, "Where *does* Tanya *live?*"
> Indirect: Peter asked where Tanya *lived.*

Questions in indirect speech which are not introduced by a question word require the introduction of whether *or* if.

> Peter asked, "Does Tanya live near here?"
> Peter asked *whether* Tanya lived near here.
> Peter asked *if* Tanya lived near here.

A. *Change the following sentences to indirect speech.*

1. I asked the clerk, "How much does this cost?"
   (*I asked the clerk how much this cost.*)
2. Mr. Carter asked me, "Where are you going?"
3. Amy asked, "Are you going to eat in the cafeteria?"
4. Roz asked, "Did you mail that letter for me?"
5. Della asked me, "Where are you going on your vacation?"
6. I asked her, "Do you like my new hat?"
7. He asked me, "How are you today?"
8. I asked the storekeeper, "What is the price of this tie?"
9. She asked me, "When will you get back from your trip?"
10. He asked her, "What time is it?"
11. The passenger asked, "When do we land?"
12. Then he asked, "Does it take longer to go by bus or by train?"
13. She asked me, "What time is it?"
14. He asked me, "How long have you studied English?"

Indirect Speech
Questions

B. *Choose the correct form.*

1. She asked me where _____ (was I, I was) going.
   *(She asked me where **I was going**.)*
2. I don't know what (is his name, his name is).
3. Ask him what time (is it, it is).
4. The mail carrier wants to know where (she lives, does she live).
5. He asked me how much (did my car cost, my car cost).
6. I don't know where (did he put, he put) those magazines.
7. He wants to know where (do we have, we have) our English lesson.
8. I wonder what time (it is, is it).
9. Ask him how old (is he, he is).
10. He asked me how old (was I, I was).
11. Find out where (does she live, she lives).
12. I asked her where (she lived, did she live).
13. We asked her whether (was she, she was) married.
14. Nathan asked me how long (had I studied, I had studied) English.
15. He didn't say where (he was, was he) going.
16. Ask him where (is Helen, Helen is).
17. I forgot where (did I put, I put) it.
18. I don't know where (does he live, he lives).
19. He asked me when (I would, would I) return.
20. Brooke asked me where (was I, I was) going.
21. I asked him what time (could he, he could) meet us.
22. The supervisor asked me why (was I, I was) late for work.

Indirect Speech
Questions

C. *Change each of the following questions to an indirect statement. Begin each one with the words given after it in parentheses.*

1. Where is the director's office? (I don't know _____.)
   *(I don't know **where the director's office is.**)*

2. Where did Miss Dale go? (He wants to know _____.)

3. What time is it? (I wonder _____.)

4. In which file is the letter? (Mr. Ames wants to know _____.)

5. How much does this cost? (I would like to know _____.)

6. How is he getting along? (The director wants to know _____.)

7. When is he leaving for the coast? (No one seems to know _____.)

8. When will Mr. Saki get back? (He asked me _____.)

9. What is the price of this book? (She said she didn't know _____.)

10. Where is he? (Do you know _____?)

11. Did he finish his test? (The teacher asked _____.)

12. Does he live in Berkeley? (Ask him _____.)

13. Where did you put it? (I forget _____.)

14. What does it mean? (I asked him _____.)

15. Where is she going? (I don't know _____.)

16. What time is he coming back? (He didn't tell me _____.)

17. Where is it? (I haven't any idea _____.)

18. Did she take it with her? (I really don't know _____.)

19. How well does she speak English? (He wants to know _____.)

20. Is he coming back today? (I'm not sure _____.)

21. Where is he going? (He didn't tell anyone _____.)

22. Did he return the book? (I don't know _____.)

Indirect Speech
Commands

Express orders or commands in indirect speech by using the infinitive form.

He said to me, "Come back later."
He told me *to come* back later.

She said to me, "Don't wait for me."
She told me not *to wait* for her.

A. *Change the following sentences from direct to indirect speech.*

1. My husband said to me, "Wait for me outside."
   *(My husband told me **to wait** for him outside.)*
2. The police officer said to us, "Don't make so much noise."
3. He told me, "Try to come on time."
4. He begged us, "Please send me some money at once."
5. He asked us, "Please sit down for a few minutes."
6. She said to me, "Don't forget what I have told you."
7. The teacher asked us, "Please be more careful when you write your reports."
8. He said to me angrily, "Don't make the same mistake again."
9. The doctor said, "Come back again tomorrow."
10. I said to him, "Don't call me again at this late hour."
11. He begged me, "Please don't mention this to Margaret."
12. I said to the boy, "Put the package inside the door."
13. The teacher said to us, "Type your compositions."
14. I said to him, "Don't ever try that trick again."

B. *Give in indirect speech what the teacher told you to do.*

1. Wait outside in the hall.
   (The teacher told me to wait outside in the hall.)
2. Stay after class.
3. Don't make so much noise.
4. Look out the window, but don't open it.
5. Stop talking to Anna.
6. Sit up straight in your seat.
7. Be quiet while I am talking.
8. Pay more attention to what I say.

Indirect Speech Review

Change the following to indirect speech.

1. She said,
   "I need a vacation."
   (She said she needed a vacation.)
   "The students need more practice in speaking."
   "These exercises are difficult for me."
   "I don't feel well."
   "Nobody can do that work as well as you."
   "I'll be back soon."
   "I may be a few minutes late."
   "I have already seen that movie."

2. He asked me,
   "When did you move here?"
   (He asked me when I moved here.)
   "Where does that girl live?"
   "How old are you?"
   "What time is it?"
   "Where are you going?"
   "How long have you studied English?"
   "Do you like to study English?"

3. I don't know,
   "When are we leaving?"
   (I don't know when we're leaving.)
   "Where does she live?"
   "What time is it?"
   "Where did they go?"
   "Does she speak English well?"
   "How long has she been studying English?"
   "What is her first name?"

4. I said to them,
   "Don't be afraid."
   (I told them not to be afraid.)
   "Wait outside for me."
   "Come back in an hour."
   "Don't mention this to anyone."
   "Do me a favor and come back later."
   "Don't go by bus."

Should, Ought To

Should *and* ought to *express obligation. (Review also page 96.) They have the same meaning and can be used interchangeably. The* contraction shouldn't *is commonly used.*

> Albert *should spend* more time studying.
> Albert *ought to spend* more time studying.
> You *shouldn't smoke* so much. You *should not smoke* so much.
> You *ought not to smoke* so much.

A. *Complete the following sentences with* should. *In negative sentences, use the contracted form.*

1. She _____ (try) to finish her projects on time.
   *(She **should try** to finish her projects on time.)*
2. They _____ not (make) so much noise.
3. I _____ (spend) more time on my English.
4. He _____ not (eat) so much.
5. You _____ (learn) as many new words as possible.
6. You _____ (ask) permission before doing it.
7. He _____ (get) more physical exercise.
8. You really _____ (go) to see a doctor.
9. Someone _____ (tell) him all about it.
10. No one _____ (spend) as much money as she does.
11. She _____ not (waste) so much time on unimportant details.
12. I _____ (write) them a letter, but I don't have anything to say.
13. You _____ not (work) so hard.
14. You _____ (rest) more and try to build up your strength.
15. We _____ (pay) more attention to what the teacher says.

B. *Complete the sentences in Exercise A with* ought to.

1. She _____ (try) to finish her projects on time.
   *(She **ought to try** to finish her projects on time.)*

Should, Ought To
Past Form

Form the past tense of should *and* ought to *with* have *and the past participle of the main verb.*

> You should study more.
> You *should have studied* more.

> He ought to finish his work.
> He *ought to have finished* his work.

Note that the past tense forms of should *and* ought to *have a negative force. They indicate that something was not done.*

A. *Change the following sentences to past time.*

1. He should study more before his exam.
   *(He **should have studied** more before his exam.*
2. You should go to the beach with us.
3. She ought to prepare her work more carefully.
4. You should type your exercises.
5. You ought not to say such things to him.
6. We ought to call him.
7. You should visit Hawaii.
8. She ought to be put in the beginner's class.
9. The letter should be sent air express.
10. You should speak to them in English.
11. They ought to buy a dog to protect the place.
12. He should tell her about it.
13. You should pay more attention to the grammar rules.
14. We should go to the beach instead of spending all day at home.
15. You ought to put some money in the bank each week.
16. You shouldn't be so generous with your money.

Should, Ought To
Past Form

B. Using the past form of should, complete the following sentences in your own words.

   1.   John went to the movies last night, but he _____.
        *(John went to the movies last night, but he **should have stayed at home and prepared his lessons**.)*

   2.   You waited for me on the corner of Juniper Street, but you _____.

   3.   He sent the letter by regular mail, but he _____.

   4.   Marsha came at eight o'clock, but she _____.

   5.   I went to the bus station to meet them, but I _____.

   6.   He gave Julie the money, but he _____.

   7.   She spoke to them in English, but she _____.

   8.   He took a business course in college, but he _____.

   9.   You prepared Lesson 10, but you _____.

   10. I watched TV last night, but I _____.

   11. Lucy put the letter on Ms. Doe's desk, but she _____.

   12. We drove to New York, but we _____.

   13. He went into business with his father, but he _____.

   14. They spent their entire vacation in London, but they _____.

   15. I called him at his office, but I _____.

   16. He invested all his money in stocks, but he _____.

   17. She gave the message to Mr. Sanders, but she _____.

   18. He spent all his money on a new car, but he _____.

C. Repeat Exercise B using the past form of ought to.

   1.   John went to the movies last night, but he _____.
        *(John went to the movies last night, but he **ought to have stayed at home and prepared his lessons**.)*

Conditional Sentences
Future Possible

A conditional sentence has two clauses, a dependent clause beginning with if *and a main clause.*

> If you study, you will pass your exam.

In a future possible conditional sentence, the dependent clause is in the present tense and the main clause is in the future tense.

> If I *have* enough money, I *shall fly* to California.

Supply the correct form of the verb in parentheses in order to make future possible conditions. Use contracted forms wherever possible.

A.

1. If Melissa studies hard, she _____ (pass) her finals.
   (If Melissa studies hard, she'll pass her finals.)
2. If I finish my work in time, I _____ (go) to the concert.
3. If I see Henry, I _____ (give) him your message.
4. If he works hard, he _____ (get) the raise.
5. If you don't hurry, we _____ (be) late for the meeting.
6. If he tries hard, he _____ (find) a job somewhere.
7. If he fails the test, he _____ (have) to repeat the course.
8. If the weather is nice tomorrow, we _____ (go) to the beach.
9. If Naomi arrives on time, I _____ (talk) to her.
10. If I have time tomorrow, I _____ (go) shopping with you.

B.

1. If I _____ (find) the book, I shall give it to you.
2. If the weather _____ (be) warm, we shall go to the park tomorrow.
3. If you _____ (turn) out the light, we shall be in the dark.
4. If you _____ (save) your money, you will be able to go on a vacation.
5. If you _____ (drive) slowly, you won't have any accidents.
6. If Jack _____ (call), I shall speak with him.
7. If you _____ (learn) how to swim, you can go with us to the beach on Sundays.

Conditional Sentences
Present Unreal

In a present unreal conditional sentence, the dependent clause is in the past tense and the main clause uses would, should, could, *or* might. *The contracted forms* 'd *and* n't *are often used.*

> If you *studied,* you *would pass* your exam.
> If you *studied,* you*'d pass* your exam.

> If I *knew* better, I *wouldn't make* these mistakes.

Supply the form of the verb in parentheses in order to form present unreal conditions. Use the full form and the contracted form.

A.

1. If I knew her well, I _____ (speak) to her.
   *(If I knew her well, I **would speak** to her. If I knew her well, I'd speak to her.)*
2. If he attended class regularly, he _____ (make) good progress.
3. If we had the money, we _____ (take) a trip to South America.
4. If he went to bed earlier, he _____ not (feel) so tired.
5. If he drove more carefully, he _____ (have) fewer accidents.
6. If John paid his debts, people _____ (respect) him more.
7. If I knew English better, I _____ (read) some English novels.
8. If he prepared his homework every night, he _____ (get) better grades.

B.

1. If I _____ (own) an automobile, I would take a trip to California.
2. If she _____ (work) harder, she would probably get a better salary.
3. If I _____ (know) how to drive, I would buy a car.
4. If Louis _____ (know) more grammar, he would make fewer mistakes.
5. If he _____ not (waste) so much time in class, he would make better progress.

Conditional Sentences
Present Unreal

Dependent clauses of present unreal conditional sentences use the past tense forms of all verbs except to be. To be *uses* were *in all persons in these clauses.*

I were	we were
you were	you were
he were	
she were	} they were
it were	

If I *were* you, I would study.
If he *were* here, he would answer your question.

Supply the form of the verb in parentheses to make present unreal conditions.

A.

1. If I _____ (be) you, I wouldn't mention it to her.
   (If I were you, I wouldn't mention it to her.)
2. If today _____ (be) Saturday, I would not have to work.
3. If I _____ (be) in your position, I would think twice before doing that.
4. If today _____ (be) a holiday, we could go to the beach.
5. If the weather _____ (be) not so hot, I am sure she would feel better.
6. If Pete _____ (be) here, he would help us with this work.
7. If you _____ (be) a millionaire, how would you spend your time?

B.

1. If George were here with us, I _____ (feel) more comfortable.
2. If they were really poor, they _____ not (be) able to live as they do.
3. If I were in Paris now, I _____ (go) to some of the summer concerts.
4. If Jill were here, she _____ (know) what to do.
5. If I were you, I _____ (tell) everyone the truth about the matter.
6. If I were a millionaire, I _____ (live) on the French Riviera.
7. If he were more ambitious, he _____ (try) to find a better job.

143

Conditional Sentences
Past Unreal

In a past unreal conditional sentence, the dependent clause is in the past perfect tense and the main clause uses would have, should have, could have, *or* might have. *The contracted forms* 'd have *and* 've *are often used.*

> If you *had studied,* you *would have passed* your exams.
> If you *had studied,* you *'d have passed* your exams.
> If you *had studied,* you *would've passed* your exams.

> If I *had known,* I *wouldn't have made* that mistake.

Supply the correct form of the verb in parentheses in order to make past unreal conditions. Use full forms and contracted forms.

A.

1. If I had known her, I _____ (speak) to her.
   *(If I had known her, I **would have spoken** to her. If I had known her, I'd have spoken to her. If I had known her, I **would've spoken** to her.)*
2. If he had learned the truth, he _____ (be) very angry.
3. If I had known that you needed me, I _____ (come) at once.
4. If they had invited us, naturally we _____ (go) to the party.
5. If you had worn your overcoat, you _____ not _____ (catch) cold.
6. If I had had your address, I _____ (write) to you.
7. If yesterday had been a holiday, I _____ (go) to the beach.
8. If you had asked me, I _____ (help) you.

B.

1. If I _____ (know) about this yesterday, I would have worried all day long.
2. If the weather _____ (be) nice yesterday, we would have gone to the beach.
3. I would have looked you up if I _____ (know) you were living in Kansas.
4. I wouldn't have gotten wet if I _____ (wear) a raincoat.
5. If he _____ (study) more, he would have gotten better grades.

Conditional Sentence Review

A. *Change the following sentences from future-possible conditions to present-unreal conditions.*

1. If Laura comes, she'll help us.
   *(If Laura **came**, she'**d help** us.)*
2. If she studies hard, she will pass her driver's test.
3. If I have the money, I shall buy a new car.
4. If I see her, I shall give her your message.
5. If you turn out the lights, we shall be in the dark.
6. If she saves her money, she will be able to go on a vacation.
7. If the weather is nice, we shall go to the beach.
8. If he has time, he will go with us.
9. If they work hard, they will learn engineering.
10. If you go to Cuba, you will have a lot of practice in speaking Spanish.
11. If Eva is present, the party will be a success.
12. If we hurry, we can get there by two o'clock.
13. If Phil works hard, he may get a better job.
14. If I don't have to study, I shall go to the movie with you.
15. If they invite me, I shall go with them.
16. If it rains, we won't go.
17. If they lend me the money, I shall be able to go into business right away.
18. If I feel better, I shall go with you.
19. If I am not busy, I shall be glad to go with you.

B. *Change the sentences in Exercise A to past-unreal conditions.*

1. If Laura comes, she'll help us.
   *(If Laura **had come**, she'**d have helped** us.)*

Conditional Sentence Review

Complete each of the following conditional sentences in your own words.

C. Present Unreal Conditions

1. I don't have a car, but if I _____.
   *(I don't have a car, but if I **had one I would drive to California on my vacation**.)*
2. I am not in Florida now, but if I _____.
3. I don't like to swim, but if I _____.
4. I don't have enough money to buy a new car, but if I _____.
5. I can't type well, but if I _____.
6. I am not in your position, but if I _____.
7. I cannot speak English perfectly, but if I _____.
8. I don't know how to play the piano, but if I _____.
9. Randy doesn't have much free time, but if he _____.
10. He never does his homework, but if he _____.
11. I am not a millionaire, but if I _____.
12. Today isn't a holiday, but if it _____.

D. Past Unreal Conditions

1. She didn't make reservations, but if she _____.
   *(She didn't make reservations, but if she **had made them, we could all have attended the grand opening**.)*
2. I didn't know your name, but if I _____.
3. Joan didn't have a car last winter, but if she _____.
4. We didn't have their phone number, but if we _____.
5. Lucille didn't get her car tuned up, but if she _____.

Conditional Sentence Review

6. I couldn't afford to take a vacation last summer, but if I _____.
7. I wasn't aware of the problem, but if I _____.
8. I couldn't speak English at that time, but if I _____.
9. He didn't study English before he came here, but if he _____.
10. He didn't come to class on time, but if he _____.
11. He didn't wear his overcoat, but if he _____.
12. There was no doctor present at the time of the accident, but if there _____.

E. *In your own words, what would you do or what would happen. . . .*

1. . . . if you never did your homework?
   (If I never did my homework, *I would fail all my tests.*)
2. . . . if you came late to class every day?
3. . . . if you found a large sum of money in the street?
4. . . . if you were unable to walk?
5. . . . if you lost your purse or wallet?
6. . . . if you found someone else's purse or wallet?
7. . . . if you failed all your exams?
8. . . . if today were a holiday?
9. . . . if you knew English perfectly?
10. . . . if you were a millionaire?
11. . . . if you were ten years younger than you are?
12. . . . if you had a lot of free time?

Conditional Sentence Review

F. *In your own words, what would you have done or what would have happened. . . .*

1. . . . if you had come to class late?
   (The teacher would have been angry *if I had come to class late.)*
2. . . . if yesterday had been a holiday?
3. . . . if you had failed all your tests last semester?
4. . . . if you had overslept this morning?
5. . . . if yesterday had been your birthday?
6. . . . if you had missed the bus this morning?
7. . . . if you had lost your purse or wallet on your way to school this morning?
8. . . . if it had been raining when you left home this morning?
9. . . . if yesterday had been Sunday?
10. . . . if you had lost your briefcase on your way to work?

G. *Complete the following conditional sentences with the proper form of the verbs in parentheses.*

1. If I were you, I _____ (tell) him the truth.
   (If I were you, I **would tell** *him the truth.)*
2. If I had been in your place, I _____ (say) this.
3. I would not have gone if I _____ (know) it was going to rain.
4. If you had called me, I _____ (be) glad to meet you.
5. If it rains next Sunday, I _____ (stay) home.
6. I shall call you next week if I _____ (want) a lesson.
7. I _____ (like) to study Spanish if I had the time.
8. I shall go to the beach next Sunday if the weather _____ (be) nice.

Conditional Sentence Review

9. If he had told me the truth, I _____ not _____ (ignore) him.
10. If he had been driving fast, it _____ (be) a more serious accident.
11. If I had worn my overcoat, I _____ not _____ (catch) cold.
12. They would not have gone if they _____ (know) it would cost so much.
13. If I were you, I _____ not (work) so hard. I_____ (be) more careful of my health.
14. If the weather is nice next Saturday, I _____ (play) tennis.
15. If we had gone out in the rain, we _____ (catch) cold.
16. I would have visited you if I _____ (know) you were living in Tucson.

H. Complete the following conditional sentences by supplying words of your own.

1. If I were you, I _____.
   (*If I were you, I* **would go home and relax.**)
2. If you had studied harder, you _____.
3. I would have gone to Philadelphia if _____.
4. I shall drive to the country Sunday if _____.
5. If I had been in your place, I _____.
6. If Sue works hard, she _____.
7. If you had asked me, I _____.
8. I would gladly have lent you the money _____.
9. If I had the time, I _____.
10. If I had known it was going to rain, I _____.
11. If it doesn't rain next Sunday, we _____.
12. If I had been in your shoes, I _____.

Present Tense
After *If, When, Until*, etc.

When dependent clauses introduced by if *describe a future possible condition (review page 141), they use the present tense. Similarly, when dependent clauses introduced by* as long as, as soon as, before, unless, until, when, *and* while *describe a future condition, they also use the present tense.*

> *If* it *rains*, we'll go inside.
> *When* it *rains*, we shall go inside.
> *As soon as* it *rains*, we'll go inside.

> *If* the telephone *rings* while I'm out, please answer it.

Supply the proper form of the verbs in parentheses.

1. We shall stay outside until it _____ (rain).
2. If the weather _____ (be) nice next Sunday, we shall go to the mountains.
3. If the workers _____ (go) on strike, production will be greatly reduced.
4. Please watch my bag while I _____ (get) my ticket.
5. Please call me as soon as you _____ (get) back from your trip.
6. I won't go unless they _____ (invite) me.
7. If the river _____ (rise) much higher, there will be a flood.
8. Don't leave until I _____ (call) you.
9. If it _____ (rain) next Saturday, I may have to cancel my trip.
10. When the weather _____ (get) warmer, we can go swimming.
11. I plan to wait here until the mail _____ (arrive).
12. If you _____ not _____ (arrive) on time, you will not get a seat.
13. When you _____ (see) the light turn red, be sure to stop your car.
14. If you _____ (sit) in the sun too long, you may get burned.
15. Give him this memorandum as soon as you _____ (see) him.

Wish

Wish *usually suggests a situation that is unreal or contrary to fact. After* wish—*as in unreal conditional statements—use a past tense clause to suggest present action and a past perfect tense clause to suggest past action.*

> Present: I *wish* she *were* here now.
>
> Past: I *wish* I had *known* about this yesterday.

The expressions I wish you would *and* I wish you wouldn't *are used to express polite commands or requests.*

> I wish you would stay here.
>
> I wish you wouldn't go home.

A. *Supply the correct form of the verbs in parentheses.*

1. I wish I _____ (own) a video recorder.
    *(I wish I **owned** a video recorder.)*
2. Ed wishes he _____ (be) a mechanical engineer.
3. I wish I _____ (go) to the movie with you last night.
4. I wish I _____ (have) today off, I'd go swimming.
5. I wish I _____ (have) yesterday off, I'd have gone swimming.
6. I wish I _____ (be) in Florida now.
7. I wish you _____ (live) nearer me.
8. I wish that, for just a day, I _____ (be) President of the United States.
9. I wish I _____ (can) help you, but I can't.
10. I wish I _____ (study) harder when I was young.

B. *Begin these imperative sentences with* I wish you would *or* I wish you wouldn't, *making them more polite.*

1. Come back in an hour.
    *(**I wish you would** come back in an hour.)*
2. Mail this letter right away, Kevin.
3. Be creative in your writing.
4. Don't make any mistakes.
5. Help me with this problem.

Too, So

In order to avoid repetition of earlier words or phrases, use too *or* so *and an appropriate auxiliary verb in affirmative sentences.*

> He speaks English and she speaks English.
>> He speaks English and she *does too.*
>> He speaks English and *so does* she.

> I went to New York and Jay went to New York.
>> I went to New York and Jay *did too.*
>> I went to New York and *so did* Jay.

A. Shorten the following sentences by using a verb phrase with too.

1. He wants to go there, and she wants to go there.
    (He wants to go there, and she does too.)
2. Liz left right after lunch, and Bob left right after lunch.
3. She is going to the concert, and I am going to the concert.
4. Kay will be here at ten o'clock, and I shall be here at ten o'clock.
5. My watch is fast, and your watch is fast.
6. She wanted to go to a movie, and I wanted to go to a movie.
7. She is making good progress, and her brother is making good progress.
8. Evan has gone back to Europe, and his wife has gone back to Europe.
9. Bert was arrested, and his assistant was arrested.
10. He saw the accident, and I saw the accident.
11. Beth liked the movie, and I liked the movie.
12. Nan will be there, and her sister will be there.
13. We go to the beach every weekend, and they go to the beach every weekend.
14. Mark can speak French, and she can speak French.
15. I have had lunch, and Cy has had lunch.

B. Shorten the sentences in Exercise A by using a verb phrase with so.

1. He wants to go there, and she wants to go there.
    (He wants to go there, and so does she.)

Either, Neither

Use either *and* neither *to avoid repetition in negative sentences.*

> He doesn't bowl, and she doesn't bowl.
>> He doesn't bowl, and she doesn't *either.*
>> He doesn't bowl, and *neither* does she.

> I didn't go to Boston, and Hal didn't go to Boston.
>> I didn't go to Boston, and Hal didn't *either.*
>> I didn't go to Boston, and *neither* did Hal.

A. *Shorten the following sentences (avoiding repetition) by using a verb phrase with* either.

1. He doesn't want to go, and she doesn't want to go.
   (He doesn't want to go, and she doesn't **either.***)*
2. Grace didn't like the movie, and I didn't like the movie.
3. She won't be here, and her sister won't be here.
4. She hasn't ever been in Europe, and I haven't ever been in Europe.
5. Lew hadn't seen the movie, and I hadn't seen the movie.
6. He would never say such a thing, and I would never say such a thing.
7. Margaret can't swim, and I can't swim.
8. He doesn't know her well, and I don't know her well.
9. Your watch isn't right, and mine isn't right.
10. I don't like to dance, and my wife doesn't like to dance.
11. Mr. Rogers wasn't at the meeting, and Mr. Barker wasn't at the meeting.
12. I couldn't hear the speaker, and my friend couldn't hear the speaker.
13. You won't enjoy that movie, and your son won't enjoy that movie.
14. We don't have a television set, and they don't have a television set.

B. *Shorten the sentences in Exercise A by using a verb phrase with* neither.

1. He doesn't want to go, and she doesn't want to go.
   (He doesn't want to go, and **neither** *does she.)*

Auxiliary Verbs

In sentences describing two opposite situations, avoid repetition with but and an appropriate auxiliary.

> She liked the movie. I didn't like the movie.
> She liked the movie, *but* I *didn't.*

> He can't speak English. His wife speaks English.
> He can't speak English, *but* his wife *can.*

A. Complete the following sentences by adding the necessary auxiliary verb.

1. She dances well, but her sister _____.
   *(She dances well, but her sister **doesn't.**)*

2. I know how to swim, but Francis _____.

3. She can speak French, but her husband _____.

4. I'll be there, but Jimmy _____.

5. They didn't like the movie, but we _____.

6. Alex agrees with you, but I_____.

7. George used to be the best student in the class, but now Ralph
   _____.

8. At first I didn't like the new manager, but now I_____.

9. Henry won't be able to attend the meeting, but Alice _____.

10. I have never been in Australia, but my wife _____.

11. Ben has seen the movie, but I_____.

12. He enjoys living in Florida, but his wife _____.

13. She knows how to swim, but her friend _____.

14. She is a serious student, but her sister _____.

15. My husband likes to golf, but I_____.

16. They are going to the beach, but I_____.

17. They don't have classes tomorrow, but we _____.

18. He knows her, but I_____.

19. Gail likes to study mathematics, but I _____.

20. She is good at mathematics, but I_____.

Auxiliary Verbs

B. *Complete the following sentences with the necessary auxiliaries.*

1. Eunice isn't going to the party, but I_____.
    (Eunice isn't going to the party, but I am.)
2. Michael will be there, but Michele_____.
3. Alexandra will go, and so _____ her husband.
4. Winnie speaks Chinese, and so _____ Penny.
5. Patrick isn't going to the party, and neither _____ his brother.
6. You say you're not going to the party, but I'm sure you _____.
7. Sandy has gone away for the summer, and so _____ Kevin.
8. Polly went to the movies last night, and Carson _____, too.
9. She isn't a good driver, and he _____ either.
10. He can't go, but I _____.
11. I can't swim, and she _____ either.
12. She says she knows him well, but I don't think she _____.
13. I knew Scotty wouldn't come, but I thought Karen _____
14. At first they thought they couldn't go, but now they think they _____.
15. She won't drive at night, but I _____.
16. At first I didn't like living in the States, but now I _____.
17. I haven't seen that play, but my daughters _____.
18. Professor Schultz can't speak German and neither _____ her husband.
19. Mr. Schultz can speak Russian; his wife _____.
20. My parents like living in California, but I _____.
21. At first the Cowboys were the best team in the league, but later on the Steelers _____.
22. Cindy doesn't want to go, and neither _____ I.

Negative Questions

Negative questions are usually formed by placing a contracted form of to be *or an auxiliary verb and* not *before the subject. When a question word is used, it is placed before the contraction.*

She is here today.	*Isn't* she here today?
Peter saw them.	*Didn't* Peter see them?
Why isn't she here today?	*Why didn't* Peter see them?

A. *Change the following sentences to negative questions. Use only contracted forms.*

1. Maurice didn't attend the meeting.
   (Didn't Maurice attend the meeting?)
2. Conrad isn't changing the oil in his car now.
3. Helene won't be here today.
4. She won't be here tomorrow either.
5. Andrea didn't take the accounting test yesterday.
6. Colleen doesn't like to study in the morning.
7. We don't like to get up early.
8. They aren't going with us to the movie tonight.
9. Mr. Donahue didn't bring the food.
10. It isn't raining.
11. It wasn't raining this morning either.
12. It hasn't rained all week.
13. The Starskys aren't moving to Cleveland.

B. *Change the sentences in Exercise A to questions beginning with* Why.

1. Maurice didn't attend the meeting.
   *(**Why** didn't Maurice attend the meeting?)*

Subject Questions

Form subject questions by substituting who, what, *or* which *for the subject of a sentence or for the modifiers of the subject.*

Stephanie lives here.	*Who* lives here?
The vase is on the table.	*What* is on the table?
The blue ribbon is his.	*Which* ribbon is his?

Change the following sentences to questions beginning with the question words in parentheses.

1. Grace broke the dish. (Who)
   *(**Who** broke the dish?)*
2. February comes before March. (Which month)
3. Coffee is one of the chief exports of Brazil. (What)
4. Lee drove the car. (Who)
5. His carelessness caused the accident. (What)
6. The red umbrella belongs to her. (Which umbrella)
7. The black notebook is hers. (Which notebook)
8. The Number 5 bus goes to the airport. (Which bus)
9. The Reillys live next door to them. (Who)
10. Mexico is south of the United States. (Which country)
11. She is the best student in the class. (Who)
12. Decreased demand causes a fall in prices. (What)
13. Bob has your book. (Who)
14. The Atlantic Ocean is east of the United States. (What ocean)
15. George won first prize in the contest. (Who)
16. This book is mine. (Which)
17. That woman is my mother. (Who)
18. Bernard is doing his homework now. (Who)

Must Have, May Have

Must have *(contracted as* must've*) indicates a strong probability that something happened in the past. It is followed by a past participle.*
May have *(no contracted form) indicates a possibility that something happened in the past. It is also followed by a past participle.*

> Samantha *must've gone* home. (She probably went home.)
> Samantha *may have gone* home. (It is possible that she went home.)

A. Supply must have *in the following sentences. Use both the full form and the contracted form. Use the past participle of the verb in parentheses.*

1. I can't find my book. I _____ (leave) it on the bus.
   *(I can't find my book. I **must have left** it on the bus. I **must've left** it on the bus.)*

2. She _____ (take) the magazine with her. It's not here.

3. They don't answer their telephone. They _____ (go) away somewhere

4. Roy _____ (study) hard before his examination.

5. She speaks English fluently. She _____ (study) a long time.

6. You _____ (see) her; she walked in front of you.

7. The bank _____ been _____ (rob) by professionals; they left no clues.

8. He _____ (come) by taxi.

B. Supply may have *in the following sentences.*

1. She _____ (take) the book by mistake.
   *(She **may have taken** the book by mistake.)*

2. They _____ (call) while you were out.

3. I_____ (leave) my keys at home or I _____ (lose) them somewhere. I'm not sure.

4. They _____ (be) wealthy at one time, but I doubt it.

5. They now think that the jewels _____ (steal) by one of the neighbors.

6. The storm _____ (delay) the plane.

Must Have, May Have

C. *Using* must have, *complete each of these sentences in your own words.*

1. They don't answer their phone; they ... .
   *(They don't answer their phone; they **must have gone** away on their vacation.)*
2. I can't find my notebook; I ... .
3. William got very good grades this semester; he ... .
4. They seem to know a lot about Latin America; they ... .
5. He speaks English very well; he ... .
6. My umbrella has suddenly disappeared; Felix ... .
7. Daphne and Mark aren't playing volleyball anymore; they ... .
8. Sam didn't attend the meeting last night; he ... .
9. The streets are wet; it ... .
10. The plan worked perfectly; they ... .

D. *Answer each of the following questions using* may have. *Add* I'm not sure *or* I don't know for sure *at the end of your answer.*

1. Did John bring his car to school today?
   *(John **may have brought** his car to school today—I'm not sure.)*
2. Did Professor Wiley learn Spanish in South America?
3. Did Helen call while I was out?
4. Was Mr. Reese born in this country or Europe?
5. Did Mary and Helen have an argument?
6. Did he pass all his exams?
7. Did Grace go shopping this afternoon?
8. Were they married in Seattle?
9. Did it rain during the night?
10. Did the New York Yankees win the World Series last year?

Causative Form

An appropriate form of to have *or* to get *plus the past participle is used to show that the subject caused someone else to perform an action.*

I often *have* my shoes *shined.*	I often *get* my shoes *shined.*
He *had* the work *done* by an expert.	He *got* the work *done* by an expert.
Did she *have* her house *painted?*	*Did* she *get* her house *painted?*

A. *Change these sentences to the causative form first with* have *and then with* get.

1. I cut my hair once a month.
   (*I **have** my hair cut once a month. I **get** my hair cut once a month.*)
2. We'll change the oil in our car soon.
3. I should clean and wax the kitchen floor.
4. You typed those letters yesterday.
5. They checked the oxygen level in their fish tank.
6. Phil is going to dry-clean his winter coat.
7. Did she repair her computer?
8. I should repair the hole in my shoes.

B. *Add a past participle plus your own words to form causative form sentences.*

1. We should have our house _____.
   (*We should have our house repainted this summer.*)
2. I'm going to get this watch _____.
3. She had her suit _____ .
4. They had their portrait _____.
5. You always get your rugs _____.
6. I wanted to have the wedding _____.
7. The twins go to Claude's to get their hair _____.
8. He always gets his teeth _____.

Exclamations

To emphasize a noun, use what *or* what a *and an exclamation point (!).*

> *What* beauty!　　*What a* beautiful painting!

To emphasize an adjective or adverb in a sentence, use how *and an exclamation point.*

> *How* fantastic!　　*How* well she swims!　　*How* tall he is!

Change these sentences to exclamations which emphasize some part of them. Use what, what a, *or* how *and an exclamation point.*

1. David reads fast.
   (***How*** *fast David reads!*)
2. It's a beautiful day.
3. He is a good-looking boy.
4. Gail plays golf well.
5. They speak English fluently.
6. Pauline is tall.
7. It is hot today.
8. It is a hot day.
9. You have good taste in clothes.
10. That's a gorgeous car.
11. She is a lucky card player.
12. We're having beautiful weather now.
13. Penny looks very old.
14. It was an interesting movie.
15. The lake is very wide.
16. That was very strange behavior.

Emphasis

Show emphasis in affirmative statements by adding do, does, *or* did *to show strong feeling. Use the simple form of the verb.*

She knows him.	She *does* know him.
I called you.	I *did* call you.

Show emphasis in imperative statements by adding do. *(Also review page 17.)*

Sit down.	*Do* sit down.

Make these sentences more emphatic by changing the italicized verb.

1. She *lives* on a houseboat. I'm sure of it.
   *(She **does live** on a houseboat. I'm sure of it.)*
2. I *wrote* that letter. I am positive of it.
3. Ed *took* the book. He told me so.
4. But we *studied* that exercise.
5. You're mistaken. I *want* to learn English.
6. I *did* it yesterday.
7. *Call* me again sometime.
8. I maintain that she *lives* in West Virginia.
9. Sam didn't visit me, but he *called* me on the phone.
10. Columbus didn't reach the Indies, but he *reached* a new continent.
11. Maps were very poor then, but they *showed* that the earth was round.
12. Rick doesn't study hard, but he *attends* class regularly.
13. I didn't go away on my vacation, but I *had* a good rest.
14. *Bring* Sue with you the next time you come.
15. *Visit* us again sometime.
16. She really *seems* to enjoy her new guitar.

Position of Prepositions

In everyday conversation, avoid beginning a question with a preposition. Put the preposition at the end of the sentence.

> What are they looking *at?*
> What country does he come *from?*

Supply the necessary prepositions at the end of these sentences.

1. What are they talking _____?
    *(What are they talking **about?**)*
2. What are you thinking _____?
3. What country was he born _____?
4. Whom (who) do you wish to speak _____?
5. What kind of car are you looking _____?
6. Whom (who) does this book belong _____?
7. What are they going to use the money _____?
8. Which restaurant do you want to eat _____?
9. Which shop did she buy the dress _____?
10. Whom (who) was the book written _____?
11. Which hotel did he go _____?
12. Whom (who) did they sell their house _____?
13. Which magazine do you want to look _____?
14. What is the guide pointing _____?
15. Which room do you have your lesson _____?
16. Where did all that dirt come _____?
17. What are you smiling _____?

Position of Prepositions

Informal usage permits moving a preposition with a relative pronoun object to the end of the sentence.

> This is the textbook *which* I was talking *about.*
> Janice was the accountant *whom* you spoke *to.*

In sentences with this construction, the relative pronoun may be dropped altogether.

> This is the textbook I was talking *about.*
> Janice was the accountant you spoke to.

A. *Change the preposition's position from before the relative pronoun to the end of the sentence or clause.*

1. This is the book about which everyone is talking.
   (This is the book which everyone is talking about.)
2. The man *to whom* you were speaking is Dr. Evans.
3. This is the room *in which* they found the clue.
4. He is the kind of salesman *from whom* it is difficult to get away.
5. The person *to whom* you should speak is Miss Williams.
6. It is a subject *on which* we shall never agree.
7. The thing *about which* they were arguing was really of little importance.
8. It is a place *in which* you feel at home.
9. It was Bob *for whom* we had to wait so long.
10. It was Liz *from whom* he borrowed the money.
11. The room *in which* we study is on the second floor.
12. This is the street *on which* they live.
13. I finally found the book *for which* I was looking.
14. The students *with whom* she studies are mainly from South America.
15. The fellow *with whom* I roomed was from Chicago.

B. *Change the position of the preposition and drop the relative pronoun in the sentences in Exercise A.*

1. This is the book *about which* everyone is talking.
   (This is the book everyone is talking about.)

Punctuation
Comma

Commas separate words, phrases, or clauses in a series.

> We need books, pencils, and chairs.
> We played tennis, took walks, and went swimming.

Commas set off days of the week, dates, addresses, and geographical names.

> He lives in Chicago, lllinois.
> It happened on Friday, October 9, 1970.

Commas set off parenthetical expressions, words in direct address, and appositives.

> He was, to be sure, an excellent diplomat.
> And so, my friends, you can see the results.
> Santini, our butcher, was hurt recently.

Punctuate the following sentences.

1. We study history mathematics geography and reading.
   (We study history, mathematics, geography, and reading.)
2. Roberta the mechanic repaired our car and also fixed our refrigerator.
3. We cannot of course reveal our sources.
4. Johnnie Reese the president of our class spent the night at our house.
5. He did not in the first place tell the whole story.
6. She was born in Scranton Pennsylvania on March 23 1953 and she has lived there ever since.
7. We cannot after all live forever.
8. By the way do you remember Zan's address?
9. Marlene Henry's cousin is visiting him at his camp in Madison Wisconsin.
10. Where were you Mr. Jones on the morning of February 12 1981?
11. The old Amos Building a famous landmark of the town was recently torn down.
    As a matter of fact it was torn down on February 12 Lincoln's birthday.
12. The most popular summer sports are tennis swimming and hiking.
13. Yesterday I met quite by accident two former schoolmates Palmer and Stewart.
14. I last saw them on graduation day June 20 1978.

Punctuation
Comma

Nonrestrictive clauses do not limit or define; they are parenthetic and are set off by commas.

> Dick, who is clever, passes all his exams.
> San Francisco, where we met, is a beautiful city.

Restrictive clauses identify or define the antecedent noun. They are not parenthetical and are not set off by commas.

> Any boy who is clever passes all his exams.
> The place where we met is a beautiful city.

Punctuate the following sentences.

1. Amy who is lazy does not deserve to pass.
   (Amy, who is lazy, does not deserve to pass.)
2. Any student who is lazy does not deserve to pass.
3. Any girl who has brown hair will be all right for the part of the heroine.
4. Mary who has brown hair was selected for the part of the heroine.
5. Little Teddy's hands which were covered with tar were very hard to clean.
6. Any passenger who enters the engine room does so at his or her own risk.
7. The man who said that is a liar.
8. Mr. Pace who told the story was obviously lying.
9. Wednesday when my brother is usually out of town will be a good day to call.
10. Mr. Hemmingway who was bored with the real estate business decided to move to Glen Acres which was formerly a swamp.
11. The man who was laughing was probably the one who played the practical joke.
12. Her hair which she painstakingly combed every morning was very neat.
13. The profit which you can expect on so cheap an article is very small.
14. We heard a noise that resembled the cry of an injured animal.
15. The George Washington Bridge which spans the Hudson River has been repaired recently.

Punctuation
Comma and Semicolon

Use a comma before a conjunction joining two independent clauses.

In the North there are many wheat fields, but cotton fields predominate in the South
We had trouble reaching him, but at last he answered.

If two independent clauses are closely related in meaning, but are not connected by a conjunction, join them with a semicolon.

In the North there are many wheat fields; in the South cotton fields predominate.
We had trouble reaching him; at last, however, he answered.

Punctuate the following sentences.

1. Chicago is my favorite city but Philadelphia has more diversity.
   (Chicago is my favorite city, but Philadelphia has more diversity.)
2. The general manager will talk to you soon and will give you the information.
3. Smith is a very good automobile mechanic and his prices are low.
4. She kept the money for more than a month and then finally returned it.
5. She kept the book for a long time but she finally returned it.
6. She kept the letters for a long time then she finally returned them.
7. There were six ambassadors and their entrance was a gaudy spectacle.
8. Andy didn't go but his wife did.
9. Maxine was pleased with the results but her husband wasn't.
10. Gloria and Edith were cautious but Archie bet on the small horse and won more than a hundred dollars.
11. Betty plays the piano and Ginger plays the violin.
12. Frank plays the saxophone Alexis plays the cornet.
13. His clothes were filthy but everyone knew that he was still the boss.
14. I got to the meeting on time but no one was there.
15. It's cold in the winter it's hot in the summer.

Punctuation Review

Punctuate the following sentences.

1. The changes which we are planning will soon be completed then we shall be able to serve you.
   (The changes which we are planning will soon be completed; then we shall be able to serve you.)

2. Jenny and Miss Smith came into the room looked around whispered to each other and then strangely enough walked out.

3. Williams store which sells many fancy groceries was recently repainted as a consequence it now looks very nice indeed.

4. I am sure Mary said William that you will like our new house which was built by that famous architect Mr James.

5. Of course Father its a pity said Ellen that people don't appreciate the excellent work which you have done here.

6. We drove from Harrisburg PA to Albany which is the capital of New York State.

7. Joan and Ellen stopped and watched Henry and Joseph running and jumping.

8. We Ida Ethel and I considered going but later we changed our collective minds and decided to stay at home and rest.

9. The man whom I saw yesterday was Ben Reeses brother Tim Reese who is an eye specialist.

10. Saturday Jan 16 1958 was the coldest day that we had had however the next day Sunday seemed even colder to me but of course I am very sensitive to cold.

11. Everyone climbed into the wagon then we started out and soon we were far out in the country it was lovely.

12. At eleven John adjourned the meeting no decision having been reached by that time.

13. I believe said the visitor that Mr. Davis should be notified at once yet we all realize naturally that the duty is not a pleasant one.

14. Cars which have emission controls are considered no good by old Dr. Reynolds who still has a 1971 Chevy.

15. Commas I noted are useful punctuation marks.

16. Come here at once I need you immediately!

17. Did you see her yesterday are you going to see her tomorrow?

18. When will we finish this exercise Robert?

Special Usage Notes

Advice/Advise

Advice *is a noun,* advise *is a verb:*

> The counselor *advised* me to take a writing course; I'll follow her *advice.*

As far as/Until

As far as *refers to distance;* until *refers to time:*

> She walked *as far as* the corner and then turned back.
> She said she could stay only *until* ten o'clock.

Beat/Win

One beats *teams or opponents; one* wins *games:*

> Tracey *won* the tennis match by *beating* Sandra in three sets.

Do/Make

The differences between these verbs are idiomatic. Both have the meaning to accomplish *or* to perform. *Note these uses:*

> This morning I *made* the bed and then *made* breakfast. Afterwards I *did* the dishes. I always *do* the housework before I *do* my exercises. I *made* a phone call, but I *made* a mistake when I dialed.

In/Into

In *suggests position within a certain space;* into *suggests action toward a certain point:*

> I made sure there was water *in* the pool before I dived *into* it.

Rob/Steal

One steals *an object; one* robs *a person or thing:*

> They *robbed* the bank and then *stole* a car to get away.

Special Usage Notes
Pour/Spill

Spill *suggests an accidental or unintentional action; pour suggests an intentional one.*

> As I was *pouring* my tea into my cup, I *spilled* some on the floor.

Choose the word in parentheses which correctly completes each sentence.

1. We rode the bus (as far as, until) the waterfront.
   (We rode the bus as far as the waterfront.)
2. I hope I don't (do, make) a mistake on my final exam.
3. What do you (advice, advise) me to do?
4. Unknowingly, she walked right (in, into) their trap.
5. My sister usually (beats, wins) me when we play Ping-Pong.
6. James tripped and (poured, spilled) his soup.
7. Yesterday someone (robbed, stole) my briefcase.
8. This class lasts (as far as, until) 9:30.
9. Stephanie is always ready to give us her (advice, advise).
10. The bartender carefully (poured, spilled) the martini from the pitcher.
11. Did the thieves (rob, steal) your parents' home again?
12. The money was already (in, into) the drawer.
13. Did you (do, make) lasagna for dinner last night?
14. Who (does, makes) the dishes in your house, you or your brother?
15. I don't usually (beat, win) when I play chess, but I'm learning.
16. I (advice, advise) you to (pour, spill) some of the milk out of that bowl in order to avoid (pouring, spilling) it.
17. Who (robbed, stole) the calculator I left (in, into) my desk?
18. He rode with me (as far as, until) Lake Ontario.
19. We walked (farther, further) and talked (farther, further).

Special Usage Notes

Beside/Besides

Beside *means* next to; besides *means* in addition to:

> *Besides* me, three others went on the trip. I sat *beside* Bart on the bus.

Few/Less

Few *is used only with plural countable nouns:* Less *is used only with noncountable nouns.*

> *few* books   *less* time
> *few* pencils   *less* sugar

Few/A few; Little/A little

Few *and* little *have a negative force and suggest the absence of some quantity or thing;* a few *and* a little *have a positive force and suggest the presence of a quantity or thing, although in small amount:*

> He has many enemies and *few* friends.
> He is not completely alone. He still has *a few* friends.

Forget/Leave

One can leave *something in a particular place, but one cannot* forget *something in a particular place:*

> I *have forgotten* my book. I *left* it at home.
> (Not: I have forgotten my book at home.)

No/Not

No *is an adjective used to modify nouns.* Not *is an adverb used to modify verbs and before* much, many, any, enough, *and any article or numeral modifying a noun:*

> She has *no* money and does *not* speak their language.
> *Not* many people came; there were probably *not* even 50 there.

Too/Very

Very *means* much *or* to a large degree. Too *always suggests* something in excess, more of something than we need or can use. Too *is often followed by an infinitive construction:*

> This book is *very* big, but it will fit in my pocket.
> This book is *too* big *to fit* in my pocket.

Special Usage Notes
Used to/To be used to (See also page 109.)

Used to *describes a habitual past action which is no longer in force. To be used to means to be accustomed to. Notice that to be used to is followed by a noun construction because the* to *in this case is not the sign of an infinitive but a preposition.*

> John *used to* study with Miss Smith.
>
> John *is used to* studying with Miss Smith and therefore doesn't wish to change teachers.

Choose the word in parentheses which correctly completes each sentence.

1. Victor spends (few, little) time on his English.
   *(Victor spends **little** time on his English.)*
2. I (am used to, used) riding on the subway; I don't mind it.
3. This soup is (too, very) hot to eat.
4. This is a (too, very) heavy chair, but I think I can move it.
5. Now that we have five children, we have (few, less) room than before.
6. Four girls (beside, besides) Sally left for camp on the bus.
7. Connie sits (beside, besides) me in my chemistry class.
8. I (left, forgot) my coat at school today.
9. There are (no, not) Eskimos in our class.
10. There are (no, not) many Eskimos in our class.
11. There is (no, not) enough support for our program; thus, we do (no, not) have the money to remain open.
12. Steve is so silly that he often (leaves, forgets) his own name.
13. That family has (few, little) money, but they still have (few, a few) acres of land which they can farm.
14. I (used, am used) to smoke cigarettes, but I stopped.
15. She made (few, little) mistakes on her test.
16. We (used to, are used to) this room and prefer not to change.
17. If people can't trust you, you will have (less, fewer) friends.
18. This bulb is (too, very) big to go into the socket.

Special Usage Notes

Borrow/Lend

One borrows *something from someone or something;* one lends *something to someone or something.*

> *Lend* me your pen, please; I only want to *borrow* it for a minute.

Despite/In spite of

Despite *and* in spite of *have the same meaning and can be used interchangeably. Note, however, that when a clause rather than a noun follows these prepositions, the construction* despite the fact *or* in spite of the fact *must be used.*

> He came *despite* the rain.
>
> He came *despite the fact* that it was raining
>
> He came *in spite of* the rain.
>
> He came *in spite of the fact* that it was raining

Speak/Talk

Speak *is used with languages, greetings, and in formal settings.* Talk *refers to a conversation and is often followed by an indirect object with* to.

> Jane *speaks* Portuguese; she'll *speak* to our group tonight.
>
> Don't *talk* during the film. If you want to *talk* to me, wait until it's over.

Teach/Learn

Learn *means to "gain knowledge";* teach *means "to instruct someone else."*

> I *learned* French last year; now I'll *teach* it to you.

Infinitives without *To*

Infinitives without to *are used after the verbs* let, make, hear, see, *and* feel.

> He *let* me *borrow* his bicycle.   She *made* us *wait* an hour.

Negative Openings

If an English sentence begins with a negative word, an auxiliary verb (or some form of to be) *must precede the subject, as in interrogative sentences.*

> *Never have* I heard such music.
>
> *Not* once *did* he mention your name.

Singular and Plural Forms in Measurements

We use the singular form of such words as foot, dollar, year, *etc., when such words are used as adjectives; we use the plural form when such words are used alone as nouns.*

> He signed a five-*year* contract.
>
> This contract runs for five *years*.

Special Usage Notes

Choose the word in parentheses which correctly completes each sentence.

1. The painters are using a twenty (feet, foot) ladder to climb up that building.
   *(The painters are using a **twenty-foot** ladder to climb up that building.)*

2. I want to (borrow, lend) your car for an hour. Will you please (borrow, lend) it to me?

3. What languages do you (speak, talk)?

4. Let's (speak, talk) about this homework assignment; it's difficult.

5. Who (taught, learned) you how to ice-skate?

6. We went for a walk (despite, despite the fact) that the weather was bad.

7. Never (I have seen, have I seen) Justin so angry.

8. Amanda is going to (teach, learn) me how to play tennis.

9. What have you (learned, taught) from your teacher this year?

10. I saw the thief (to take, take) the money.

11. Not once (the speaker mentioned, did the speaker mention) the subject of foreign aid.

12. The doctor made us (wait, to wait) two hours in her office.

13. Nowhere (you could find, could you find) a more generous person.

14. Kareem is a seven (feet, foot) tall basketball player. When he was fifteen years old he was already six (feet, foot) tall.

15. (In spite of, in spite of the fact) that he was ill, Gerald attended each session of the conference.

16. I haven't heard them (make, to make) a sound for hours.

17. How long did Professor Morgan (talk, speak) at the dinner last night?

18. My sister never has enough money; she is always (lending, borrowing) some from me until her next paycheck.

19. We need to discuss the matter (farther, further).

Appendix

Principal Parts of Common Irregular Verbs

Present	Past	Past Participle	Present	Past	Past Participle
arise	arose	risen	fall	fell	fallen
awake	awoke	awakened	feed	fed	fed
bear	bore	born	feel	felt	felt
beat	beat	beaten	fight	fought	fought
become	became	become	find	found	found
begin	began	begun	fling	flung	flung
bend	bent	bent	fly	flew	flown
bet	bet	bet	forget	forgot	forgotten
bind	bound	bound	forgive	forgave	forgiven
bite	bit	bitten	freeze	froze	frozen
bleed	bled	bled	get	got	gotten
blow	blew	blown	(got)		
break	broke	broken	give	gave	given
bring	brought	brought	go	went	gone
build	built	built	grind	ground	ground
burst	burst	burst	grow	grew	grown
cast	cast	cast	hang	hung	hung
catch	caught	caught	have	had	had
choose	chose	chosen	hear	heard	heard
cling	clung	clung	hide	hid	hidden
come	came	come	hit	hit	hit
cost	cost	cost	hold	held	held
creep	crept	crept	hurt	hurt	hurt
cut	cut	cut	keep	kept	kept
dare	dared	dared	know	knew	known
deal	dealt	dealt	lay	laid	laid
dig	dug	dug	lead	led	led
do	did	done	leave	left	left
draw	drew	drawn	lend	lent	lent
dream	dreamed	dreamed	let	let	let
	(dreamt)	(dreamt)	lie	lay	lain
drink	drank	drunk	light	lit	lit
drive	drove	driven	(lighted)	(lighted)	
eat	ate	eaten	lose	lost	lost

Principal Parts of Common Irregular Verbs
(Continued)

Present	Past	Past Participle	Present	Past	Past Participle
make	made	made	spend	spent	spent
mean	meant	meant	spin	spun	spun
meet	met	met	split	split	split
owe	owed	owed	spread	spread	spread
pay	paid	paid	spring	sprang	sprung
quit	quit	quit	stand	stood	stood
read	read	read	steal	stole	stolen
ride	rode	ridden	stick	stuck	stuck
ring	rang	rung	sting	stung	stung
rise	rose	risen	strike	struck	struck
run	ran	run	string	strung	strung
see	saw	seen	swear	swore	sworn
seek	sought	sought	sweep	swept	swept
sell	sold	sold	swim	swam	swum
send	sent	sent	swing	swung	swung
set	set	set	take	took	taken
shake	shook	shaken	teach	taught	taught
shave	shaved	shaved	tear	tore	torn
shine	shone	shone	tell	told	told
shoot	shot	shot	think	thought	thought
show	showed	shown	throw	threw	thrown
		(showed)	understand	understood	understood
shrink	shrank	shrunk	wake	woke	woke
shut	shut	shut	wear	wore	worn
sing	sang	sung	weave	wove	woven
sink	sank	sunk	wed	wed	wed
sit	sat	sat	weep	wept	wept
sleep	slept	slept	wet	wet	wet
slide	slid	slid	win	won	won
slit	slit	slit	wind	wound	wound
speak	spoke	spoken	wring	wrung	wrung
speed	sped	sped	write	wrote	written

Sample Conjugations
Irregular Verb: to be

Present Tense

I am	we are
you are	you are
he, she, it is	they are

Past Tense

I was	we were
you were	you were
he, she, it was	they were

Future Tense

I shall be	we shall be
you will be	you will be
he, she, it will be	they will be

Present Perfect Tense

I have been	we have been
you have been	you have been
he, she, it has been	they have been

Past Perfect Tense

I had been	we had been
you had been	you had been
he, she, it had been	they had been

Future Perfect Tense

I shall have been	we shall have been
you will have been	you will have been
he, she, it will have been	they will have been

Sample Conjugations
(Continued)
Regular Verb: to work (simple form)

Present Tense	
I work	we work
you work	you work
he, she, it works	they work

Past Tense	
I worked	we worked
you worked	you worked
he, she, it worked	they worked

Future Tense	
I shall work	we shall work
you will work	you will work
he, she, it will work	they will work

Present Perfect Tense	
I have worked	we have worked
you have worked	you have worked
he, she, it has worked	they have worked

Past Perfect Tense	
I had worked	we had worked
you had worked	you had worked
he, she, it had worked	they had worked

Future Perfect Tense	
I shall have worked	we shall have worked
you will have worked	you will have worked
he, she, it will have worked	they will have worked

Sample Conjugations
(Continued)

Regular Verb: to work (continuous form)

Present Tense

I am working	we are working
you are working	you are working
he, she, it is working	they are working

Past Tense

I was working	we were working
you were working	you were working
he, she, it was working	they were working

Future Tense

I shall be working	we shall be working
you will be working	you will be working
he, she, it will be working	they will be working

Present Perfect Tense

I have been working	we have been working
you have been working	you have been working
he, she, it has been working	they have been working

Past Perfect Tense

I had been working	we had been working
you had been working	you had been working
he, she, it had been working	they had been working

Future Perfect Tense

I shall have been working	they will have been working
you will have been working	you will have been working
he, she, he, it will have been working	they will have been working

Sample Conjugations
(Continued)

Irregular Verb: to see (passive voice)

Present Tense

I am seen	we are seen
you are seen	you are seen
he, she, it is seen	they are seen

Past Tense

I was seen	we were seen
you were seen	you were seen
he, she, it was seen	they were seen

Future Tense

I shall be seen	we shall be seen
you will be seen	you will be seen
he, she, it will be seen	they will be seen

Present Perfect Tense

I have been seen	we have been seen
you have been seen	you have been seen
he, she, it has been seen	they have been seen

Past Perfect Tense

I had been seen	we had been seen
you had been seen	you had been seen
he, she, it had been seen	they had been seen

Future Perfect Tense

I shall have been seen	we shall have been seen
you will have been seen	you will have been seen
he, she, it will have been seen	they will have been seen

Answers to Exercises

Page 1   2. are 3. am 4. is 5. are 6. is 7. is 8. are 9. are 10. am 11. is 12. are 13. is 14. are 15. is 16. are

Page 2   A-B. 2. You are not angry.-Are you angry? 3. He and she are not cousins.-Are he and she cousins? 4. He is not very serious.-Is he very serious? 5. Both sisters are not tall.-Are both sisters tall? 6. She is not a clever woman.-Is she a clever woman? 7. They are not members of the country club.-Are they members of the country club? 8. He is not a good tennis player.-Is he a good tennis player? 9. Elaine is not a pilot with American Airlines.-Is Elaine a pilot with American Airlines? 10. The sky is not very cloudy today.-Is the sky very cloudy today? 11. The office of the supervisor is not on the first floor.-Is the office of the supervisor on the first floor? 12. It is not cold today.-Is it cold today? 13. She is not in her office.-Is she in her office? 14. It is not a good movie.-Is it a good movie? 15. The stamps are not in my desk.-Are the stamps in my desk? 16. He is not a smart man.-Is he a smart man?

Page 3   A. salesmen, buzzes, oranges, dishes, glasses, players, feet B. 2. The glasses are in the kitchen. 3. They are new dishes. 4. The buses are at the corner. 5. The children are in the garden. 6. The clocks are on the wall. 7. The watches are new. 8. They are good pictures. 9. They are young men. 10. They are young women. 11. The dishes are broken. 12. The taxes are high.

Page 4   2. an 3. an 4. an 5. a, an 6. a 7. an 8. a 9. a 10. a 11. an 12. a 13. an 14. an 15. an 16. a 17. a 18. a

Page 5   2. has 3. have 4. has 5. have 6. has 7. has 8. have 9. have 10. has 11. has 12. have 13. have 14. has 15. has 16. have 17. has 18. has 19. have 20. have

Page 6   2. come 3. walk 4. play 5. eat 6. works 7. like 8. chases 9. works 10. sits 11. play 12. cook 13. eat 14. ride 15. take 16. travel 17. attend 18. speaks

Page 7   2. does 3. try 4. tries 5. wishes 6. teaches 7. go 8. watch 9. plays 10. studies 11. watches 12. kisses 13. catch 14. catches 15. does 16. carries

Page 8   B-C-D. 2. He works hard. They work hard. She works hard. 3. He's a good employee. They are good employees. She's a good employee. 4. He owns a-They own a-She owns a 5. He's an American. They're Americans. She's an American. 6. He enjoys each-They enjoy each-She enjoys each 7. He wants to-They want to -She wants to 8. He has a new wristwatch. They have new wristwatches. She has a new wristwatch. 9. He speaks-They speak-She speaks 10. He wishes to-They wish to-She wishes to 11. He reads-They read-She reads 12. He passes-They pass-She passes 13. He always goes-They always go-She always goes 14. He tries-They try-She tries 15. He does-They do-She does 16. He plays-They play-She plays 17. He has-They have-She has 18. He always sits at this desk. They always sit at these desks. She always sits at this desk. 19. He does his-They do their-She does her 20. He studies-They study-She studies

Page 9   2. The knives are 3. The dishes are 4. We have new pens. 5. The planes leave 6. The buses stop 7. The boxes are 8. The churches are 9. The offices open 10. The men know the lessons well. 11. We enjoy 12. They are 13. The boys do 14. The women are 15. The glasses are 16. The watches run 17. The clerks are 18. The keys are

Page 10   2. my 3. her 4. my 5. your 6. their 7. his 8. our 9. her 10. its, its 11. their 12. my 13. its 14. their 15. your 16. our 17. her

Page 11   There is 3. There are 4. There is 5. There are 6. There are 7. There is 8. There are 9. There is 10. There is 11. There are 12. There are 13. There is 14. There is 15. There are 16. There are

Page 12   A-B. 2. There aren't two-Are there two 3. There isn't a-There is 4. There aren't two-Are there two 5. There isn't a-Is there a 6. There aren't several-Are there several 7. THere aren't ten now-Are there ten now-8. There isn't a-Is there a 9. There aren't enough-Are there enough 10 There aren't plenty-Are there plenty 11. There isn't a-Is there a 12. There isn't a-Is there 13. There aren't telephones-Are there telephones 14. There are four-Are there four

Page 13   2. Macy's 3. Chicago's 4. men's 5. ladies' 6. child's 7. children's 8. Bob's 9. doctor's 10. Smith's 11. Lincoln's 12. Sally's 13. Jackson's 14. St. Peter's, St. Paul's

Page 14   2. These rooms are 3. Those pens... are 4. These stacks... belong 5. Those boys... are 6. Those books are 7. Those purses... are 8. These are... chairs 9. Those are... pens 10. These messages are 11. Those letters... are 12. These are my pens 13. Those mountains... form 14. These cars belong 15. Those offices... are... offices 16. These chairs are

Page 15   2. us 3. her 4. us 5. me 6. them 7. him 8. him 9. us 10. me 11. us 12. Them 13. her 14. He 15. me 16. us 17. her 18. me 19. me 20. them

Page 16   2. them 3. her 4. you 5. them 6. them 7. us 8. them 9. him 10. her 11. them 12. him 13. him or her 14. him or her 15. her 16. them 17. him 18. them 19. them 20. them

Page 17   A-B-C 2. Give this-Don't give this-Please give this 3. Open-Don't open-Please open 4. Close-Don't close-Please close 5. Wait-Don't Wait-Please wait 6. Call-Don't call-Please call 7. Let-Don't let-Please let 8. Let-Don't let-Please let 9. Turn off-Don't turn off-Please turn off 10. Put-Don't put-Please put 11. Drop-Don't drop-Please drop 12. Leave-Don't leave-Please leave 13. Let-Don't let-Please let 14. Help-Don't help-Please help 15. Send-Don't send-Please send

Page 18   2. Ella does not like, Ella doesn't like 3. You do not speak, You don't speak 4. The plane does not leave, The plane doesn't leave 5. He does not know, He doesn't know 6. I do not feel, I don't feel 7. He does not eat, He doesn't eat 8. She does not always come, She doesn't always come 9. They do not live, They don't live 10. We do not need, We don't need 11. Janet and I do not cook, Janet and I don't study 12. I do not understand, I don't understand 13. She does not want, She doesn't want 14. He does not begin, He doesn't begin 15. The child does not play, The child doesn't play 16. Gina and James do not make, Gina and James don't make 17. It does not rain, It doesn't rain 18. You do not own, You don't own

Page 19   2. Do they enjoy 3. Does that company buy 4. Does it look 5. Does he drive 6. Does the committee meet 7. Does he seem to be 8. Does this book belong 9. Do you like 10. Do you speak 11. Does he often go 12. Do I take 13. Do they sell 14. Does the store open 15. Does it close 16. Does he eat 17. Does she live 18. Do he and I sing 19. Do Tony and his mother play

Page 20   2. do 3. does 4. does 5. do 6. does 7. do 8. does 9. do 10. does 11. does 12. do 13. does 14. does, does 15. do 16. do 17. does 18. do 19. do 20. do 21. does 22. do

Page 21   2. What time does the play begin? 3. When do they get home every night? 4. How well does the travel agent speak French? 5. How much do those books cost? 6. How do they travel? 7. How often does he come here? 8. How does she feel? 9. Why does Francine want to learn English? 10. Where do they meet every morning? 11. How often do we go to the movies? 12. Where does the banker go after the play? 13. How many new words do we learn every day? 14. Where do they eat lunch? 15. What kind of car does he drive? 16. Where does this plate belong? 17. In which room does the committee meet? 18. What does she teach us? 19. When does it rain? 20. What time does he get up every morning? 21. When does she go to bed?

Page 22   2. was 3. were 4. was 5. were 6. was 7. were 8. were 9. were 10. was 11. were 12. was. was 13. was 14. were 15. were 16. were 17. were 18. was

Page 23   A-B. 2. These doors were not-These doors weren't-Were these doors closed? 3. The exercises were not-The exercises weren't-Were the exercises easy to do? 4. The man was not-The man wasn't-Was the man a stranger to her? 5. It was not-It wasn't-Was it a pleasant day? 6. The sea was not-The sea wasn't-Was the sea very rough? 7. He was not-He wasn't-Was he a tall man? 8. There were not-There weren't-Were there ten new words in the lesson? 9. Sarah was not-Sarah wasn't-Was Sarah a good swimmer? 10. She was not-She wasn't-Was she very intelligent? 11. They were not-They weren't-Were they both Americans? 12. She was not-She wasn't a-Was she a good tennis player? 13. You were not-You weren't-Were you a happy child? 14. He was not-He wasn't-Was he always angry? 15. They were not-They weren't-Were they friendly enemies? 16. Bert was not-Bert wasn't-Was Bert an old friend of the family?

Page 24   2. listened 3. talked 4. wanted 5. lived 6. expected 7. lasted 8. changed 9. liked 10. waited 11. painted 12. arrived 13. watched 14. studied 15. mailed 16. learned 17. married.

Page 25   2. told 3. sat 4. put 5. began 6. wrote 7. saw 8. cost 9. ate 10. drank 11. gave, told 12. sold 13. heard 14. knew, came 15. felt 16. went, got 17. read 18. had 19. spoke

Page 26   2. You did not tell-You didn't tell 3. He did not put-He didn't put 4. They did not stay-They didn't stay 5. Judy and I did not see-Judy and I didn't see 6. He did not plan-He didn't plan 7. The meeting did not last-The meeting didn't last 8. The book did not cost-The book didn't cost 9. The woman and her husband did not work-The woman and her husband didn't work 10. I did not know-I didn't know 11. They did not sell-They didn't sell 12. I did not speak-I didn't speak 13. She did not come-She didn't come 14. We did not sit-We didn't sit 15. I did not go-I didn't go 16. You did not give-You didn't give

Page 27   2. Did he give 3. Did they stay 4. Did she tell 5. Did you move 6. Did Terry fly 7. Did we go 8. Did they come 9. Did Carla and Dave know 10. Did he work 11. Did she feel 12. Did the meeting begin 13. Did I pass 14. Did they put 15. Did I give 16. Did the crowd wait

Page 28   2. When did they sell their home? 3. What time did the meeting begin? 4. How much did the tickets cost? 5. How did he pay for the car? 6. How much did she invest in the stock market? 7. In which row did they sit? 8. In what language did he speak to them? 9. How long did the meeting last? 10. What time did it begin? 11. What time did I telephone her? 12. Why did he go to Denver? 13. How many times did you mention it to him? 14. Where did they eat lunch? 15. How many years did we work there? 16. Where did I put the mail? 17. How long did she wait for them? 18. What time did we get home? 19. Who did he walk to the meeting with? 20. Where did you go after the lesson?

Page 29　2. hard 3. quickly 4. slowly 5. slowly 6. slow 7. rapidly 8. permanent 9. permanently 10. easy 11. easily 12. hard 13. fast 14. serious 15. seriously 16. completely 17. soft 18. softly 19. beautiful 20. beautifully

Page 30　2. well 3. good 4. well 5. good 6. good 7. well 8. Well 9. well 10. good 11. well, good 12. good 13. well 14. good 15. good 16. well 17. good 18. well 19. well 20. good 21. well 22. good

Page 31　A-B-C. 2. There aren't eleven-Are there eleven-How many months are there in a year? 3. The plane didn't arrive-Did the plane arrive-When did the plane arrive? 4. It isn't-Is it-What time is it now? 5. He didn't go-Did he go-How did he go to Chicago? 6. The two boys aren't-Are the two boys-Where are the two boys? 7. The magazine didn't cost-Did the magazine cost-How much did the magazine cost? 8. They don't live-Do they live-Where do they live now? 9. They didn't live-Did they live-How long did they live in France? 10. He didn't get up-Did he get up-What time did he get up this morning? 11. They didn't sit-Did they sit-How long did they sit in the park? 12. She doesn't speak-Does she speak-What language does she speak? 13. The meeting doesn't begin-Does the meeting begin-What time does the meeting begin? 14. She doesn't drink-Does she drink How many cups of coffee does she drink every day? 15. They didn't begin-Did they begin-When did they begin to work? 16. I'm not-Am I-How old am I? 17. They don't plan-Do they tried plan-When do they plan to finish the work? 18. We didn't get-Did we get-When did we get sick? 19. The stores weren't closed-Were the stores closed-Why were the stores closed? 20. There weren't-Were there-How many employees were absent from work this morning? 21. You don't usually travel-Do you usually travel-How do you usually travel? 22. Mary didn't deliver-Did Mary deliver-When did Mary deliver the merchandise? 23. Scotty and Karen didn't eat-Did Scotty and Karen eat-Where did Scotty and Karen eat dinner?

Page 32　2. brought 3. forgot 4. became 5. made 6. lost, found 7. fought 8. rang 9. sent 10. thought 11. taught 12. bought, sold 13. kept, gave 14. did, caught 15. sang, understood 16. stood 17. broke, took

Page 33　2. wrote 3. forgot 4. arrived 5. answered 6. made 7. rang 8. waited 9. went, rang 10. cost 11. tried 12. had 13. planned 14. took 15. sent 16. needed, bought 17. spoke 18. told, had 19. broke 20. thought 21. was 22. knew 23. understood, spoke

Page 34　A. 2. She brought me the magazines. 3. She sent them flowers. 4. He told us the whole story. 5. I cooked Victoria dinner. 6. We wrote them several letters. 7. I took her the presents. 8. He sold a friend his property. 9. He gave each child a piece of the candy. 10. Don't show anyone these pictures. 11. He bought his wife several new dresses. 12. They sent us some postcards from South America.

　　　B. 2. I sent many presents to her. 3. Please hand that magazine to me. 4. Don't tell the news to her yet. 5. You made a sweater for your sister. 6. Don't show these things to Flo. 7. He wrote a letter to me on Wednesday. 8. She told the whole story to us. 9. The teacher gives too much homework to us. 10. You made a promise to me that you must keep.

Page 35   2. that 3. who 4. who 5. which 6. whom 7. whom 8. that 9. that 10. that 11. which 12. who 13. who 14. that

Page 36   2. She will be 3. Ms. Kobolski and you will be 4. They will both be 5. This will be 6. There will be 7. We shall be 8. I shall be 9. He will be 10. The dog will be 11. Mr. Pate will be 12. Business will be 13. The exercises will be 14. There will be 15. The cafeteria will be 16. We shall be 17. You will be 18. The highway will be

Page 37   2. They will, They'll see 3. I shall, I'll give 4. She will, She'll help 5. Mary will, Mary'll clean off 6. The stores will, The stores'll close 7. I shall, I'll leave 8. Helen will, Helen'll find 9. You will, You'll spend 10. John will, John'll do 11. The wind will, The wind'll blow 12. We shall, We'll meet 13. I shall, I'll pay 14. You will, You'll learn 15. We shall, We'll remain

Page 38   2. We shall not tell-We won't tell 3. I shall not be-I won't be 4. The weather will not be-The weather won't be 5. He will not be able to meet-He won't be able to meet 6. These exercises will not be-These exercises won't be 7. We shall not eat-We won't eat 8. You will not get tired-You won't get tired 9. We shall not be there-We won't be there 10. I shall not do-I won't do 11. They will not sign-They won't sign 12. They will not finish-They won't finish 13. The meeting will not last-The meeting won't last 14. The stores will not close-The stores won't close 15. It will not cost-It won't cost 16. We shall not be ready-We won't be ready

Page 39   A-B. 2. Shall I be back-When shall I be back? 3. Will the stores be-How late will the stores be open? 4. Will it cost-How much will it cost to fix the lamp? 5. Will the plant die-Why will the plant die? 6. Will they spend-How much time will they spend in France? 7. Will she meet us-Where will she meet us? 8. Will they pay-When will they pay their bill? 9. Will the meeting begin-When will the meeting begin? 10. Will it last-How long will it last? 11. Will she leave a-What will she leave on the table for him? 12. Will you return-When will you return? 13. Will there be-How many new members will there be in the club? 14. Will the meeting be-When will the meeting be over? 15. Will they write to us-When will they write to us? 16. Will he take-Where will he take the children? 17. Shall I pass-What shall I pass? 18. Shall we stay-Where shall we stay?

Page 40   2. for, in 3. in 4. for, in 5. for 6. at 7. in 8. into 9. of, on 10. about, in 11. to 12. to, for 13. in, of 14. along 15. at 16. at 17. for, in 18. for 19. on 20. about, to 21. at, about 22. up, on 23. to, on 24. from 25. up

Page 41   Students use their own words.

Page 42   2. It took me an hour to finish my work. 3. It took her only one year to learn to speak English well. 4. It took me thirty minutes to write my paper. 5. It took the train three hours to go around the mountain. 6. It took them one year to finish the bridge. 7. I took the cable two days to reach him. 8. It takes us about fifteen minutes to walk to school every morning. 9. It will take you about an hour to get there. 10. It will take us two hours to paint the bathroom. 11. It'll take you only 1 1/2 hours to paint the kitchen. 12. It takes me less than fifteen minutes to wash and dress each morning. 13. It takes him half an hour to put on his makeup. 14. It took him just a few days to learn to swim. 15. It took her two months to recover from her illness. 16. It will take me just two or three minutes to run to the corner store and get what you need.

Page 43   2. paid 3. shook, said 4. blew 5. threw, hit 6. slept 7. met 8. found 9. wore

10. cut, ran 11. drove 12. lent, spent 13. held 14. won, lost 15. shut, locked, went 16. rode

Page 44 2. is stopping 3. is ringing 4. are wearing 5. is beginning 6. is knocking 7. is sleeping 8. is trying 9. is doing 10. are beginning 11. is having 12. is playing 13. are traveling 14. is acting 15. are having 16. are flying 17. are growing 18. are doing

Page 45 2. meets 3. is teaching, is substituting 4. rings, is ringing 5. is watching watches 6. is knocking 7. comes 8. am reading 9. blows 10. is acting 11. is having 12. is studying 13. get 14. stays, comes, is staying 15. rises, is rising 16. are building

Page 46 A-B. 2. It isn't beginning-Is it beginning 3. The sky isn't getting-Is the sky getting 4. She isn't working-Is she working 5. The maid isn't cleaning-Is the maid cleaning 6. They aren't taking-Are they taking 7. You aren't having-Are you having 8. John isn't doing-Is John doing 9. We aren't laughing-Are we laughing 10. They aren't traveling-Are they traveling 11. I'm not taking-Am I taking 12. The leaves aren't beginning-Are the leaves beginning 13. All the birds aren't flying-Are all the birds flying 14. Ellen isn't writing-Is Ellen writing 15. They aren't planning-Are they planning 16. He isn't looking-Is he looking

Page 47 2. They're 3. I'll 4. She's 5. It's 6. She'll 7. We're 8. They're 9. It's 10. We're 11. You'll 12. It's 13. There's 14. They'll 15. He's 16. You're 17. I'm 18. There 's 19. He'll 20. It'll

Page 48 2. They don't 3. She isn't 4. He isn't 5. They aren't 6. He doesn't 7. You didn't 8. She doesn't 9. You aren't 10. We weren't 11. George wasn't 12. She and her husband don't 13. I won't 14. There weren't 15. They won't 16. You aren't 17. They aren't

Page 49 2. a 3. a 4. The 5. a 6. The 7. The 8. A 9. a 10. The 11. a 12. The 13. a 14. The 15. a

Page 50 No Exercises

Page 51 2. The 3. The 4. the, the 5. the 6. -, - 7. - 8. - 9. The 10. The, the, the 11. -, the, the 12. the 13. the -, -, -, - 14. -, a, - 15. -, -, the, - 16. The, the 17. - 18. The, the 19. - 20. the, the 21. - 22. the. 23. -

Page 52 2.-, the 3. the (a), the, 4. -, the, the 5. The, -6. -, the, the, -7. The, the, -, -8. The, -9. -, -, the 10. The 11. The, the, the, the 12. The, -13. -, - - 14. The, -, the 15. The 16. The, a - 17. The,-

Page 53 2. The, the, the 3. a, a, a, a, the 4. -, the (a) -5. the, -, -, -6. a, the 7. The, -, the, - 8. the, the, -9. -, The 10. -, the, the 11. the, the 12. The, the 13. the, The 14.-, the 15.-,-,-,-,- 16.-,

Page 54 2. We are going to eat-We're going to eat 3. I am going to leave-I'm going to leave 4. They are going to wait-They're going to wait 5. We are going to get up-We're going to get up 6. She is going to drive-She's going to drive 7. We are going to go-We're going to go 8. You are going to have-You're going to have 9. They are going to go-They're going to go 10. Mike is going to take-Mike's going to take 11. It is going to be-It's going to be 12. it is going to rain-it's going to rain 13. Henry is going to study-Henry's going to study 14. You are going to stay-You're going to stay 15. Mr. and Mrs. Blake are going to build-Mr. and Mrs. Blake're going to build 16. He is going to start-He's going to start 17. They are going to move-They're going to move 18. It is going to be-It's going to be

Page 55 2. We were going (We were going to go) 3. I was going to 4. They were going to 5. We were going (We were going to go) 6. You were going to 7. They were going to 8. he was going to 9. I was going to 10. I was going to 11. They were going to 12. she was going to 13. We were going (We were going to go) 14. I was going to

Page 56 2. is coming 3. are, going, is going 4. is sailing 5. is, coming 6. is leaving 7. am going 8. is arriving 9. are, going, Is, going 10. is leaving 11. are coming 12. is going, is, going 13. is, arriving 14. is coming 15. is flying 16. am leaving 17. is, leaving

Page 57 2. You may not.... 3. We should not, We shouldn't.... 4. He may not.... 5. They cannot, They can't.... 6. We must not, We mustn't.... 7. I cannot, I can't.... 8. She should not, She shouldn't.... 9. We must not, We mustn't.... 10. She cannot, She can't.... 11. He cannot, He can't.... 12. You should not, You shouldn't.... 13. She may not.... 14. You cannot, You can't.... 15. You may not....

Page 58 2. Can they both speak English well? 3. Should Betsy spend more time on her English? 4. May we sit in these chairs? 5. Can they meet us at two o'clock? 6. May I call you later? 7. Should he eat less meat? 8. May he tell her with her lessons? 9. Should we speak to her about it? 10. May they leave now? 11. Could you go by plane? 12. Could you send them a fax? 13. Should I stay at home more? 14. May Allan wait in his office? 15. Can Al go with us to the beach? 16. Could she leave immediately?

Page 59 2. Where could the baby-sitter wait? 3. Where may you study? 4. How sick is he? 5. How well can I understand English? 6. What time should you be here? 7. Why should we tell her about it? 8. Where can he meet us? 9. How tall is Lew? 10 Where are they? 11. Why should I tell her the truth? 12. What time must you be here? 13. Where should Karen sit? 14. What kind of person is he? 15. What time is it? 16. Why are both engineers absent from work today?

Page 60 A-B. 2. Yes, I do. No, I don't. 3. Yes, he/she does. No, he/she doesn't. 4. Yes, he/she does. No, he/she doesn't. 5. Yes, I shall. No, I won't. 6. Yes, he will. No, he won't. 7. Yes, I am. No, I'm not. 8. Yes, it is. No, it isn't. 9. Yes, it does. No, it doesn't. 10. Yes, it is. No, it isn't. 11. Yes, it is. No, it isn't. 12. Yes, I did. No, I didn't. 13. Yes, I did. No, I didn't. 14. Yes, it is. No, it isn't. 15. Yes, it was. No, it wasn't. 16. Yes, he/she did. No, he/she didn't. 17. Yes, it is. No, it isn't. 18. Yes, it was. No, it wasn't. 19. Yes, it will. No, it won't. 20. Yes, you may. No, you may not. 21. Yes, I can. No, I can't. 22. Yes, it did. No, it didn't. 23. Yes, I did. No, I didn't. 24. Yes, I was. No, I wasn't. 25. Yes, I will. No, I won't. 26. Yes, it is. No, it isn't

Page 61 2. older than 3. bigger than 4. better than 5. worse than 6. easier than 7. more valuable than 8. more attractive than 9. more often than 10. more frequently than 11. earlier than

Page 62 2. more carefully than 3. harder than 4. longer than 5. more bravely than 6. more quickly than 7. more loudly than 8. sooner than 9. warmer than 10. more expensive than 11. more satisfactory than 12. wider than 13. more difficult than 14. better than 15. cleverer than 16. hotter than 17. more rapidly than

Page 63 2. the most expensive 3. the worst 4. the most important 5. the hardest 6. the most ambitious 7. the earliest 8. the most gracefully 9. the most intelligent 10. the funniest 11. the coldest 12. the best

Page 64 2. was raining 3. was having 4. were traveling 5. was sleeping 6. was just ordering 7. were driving 8. was working 9. was just taking 10. was talking 11. were traveling 12. was getting 13. was traveling

Page 65 3. I was going 4. I went 5. We drove 6. We were driving 7. We were having 8. We had 9. I was coming 10. I came 11. wind was blowing 12. wind blew 13. It rained 14. It was raining 15. sun was shining 16. sun shone 17. I was reading 18. I read 19. I was sleeping 20. I slept 21. June was playing

Page 66 2. was raining, left 3. fell, hurt, was riding 4. called, were having 5. started, was living 6. were sitting, drove 7. was getting off, slipped, broke 8. was driving, happened 9. came, was leaving 10. were leaving, called 11. was talking, saw 12. telephoned, was working

Page 67 Students use their own words to complete the sentences. 2. I was talking 3. Tony was walking 4. She was eating 5. I was finishing 6. Larry was speaking 7. I was writing 8. He was living 9. They were getting off 10. We were having 11. Chris was leaving 12. Dr. Berger was having 13. Sharon was typing 14. I was visiting 15. The puppy was crying

Page 68 2. shall be traveling 3. shall be having 4. shall be waiting 5. will be practicing 6. will be raining 7. shall be working 8. shall be flying 9. will be watching 10. will be taking 11. will be studying

Page 69 A. 2. much 3. many 4. much 5. much 6. much 7. many 8. many 9. much 10. much 11. many 12. many 13. much 14. many 15. much 16. much 17. many 18. many
  B. Sentences 2, 3, 4, 5, 6, 7, 8, 9, 14, 15, 16, 18

Page 70 A. 2. John doesn't like to play tennis either. 3. They don't want to move to the suburbs either. 4. Richard won't come either. 5. He doesn't eat in that restaurant either. 6. We can't play baseball either. 7. He doesn't like American food either. 8. She isn't able to hear him either. 9. My parents don't like to listen to the radio either. 10. Mr. Johnson isn't a tennis player either. 11. Molly can't play this game either. 12. This book wasn't expensive either.

  B. 2. She also likes to watch television.-She likes to watch television too. 3. Helen can also swim well.-Helen can swim well too. 4. The manager was also able to speak to him.-The principal was able to speak to him too. 5. They also want to live in the suburbs.-They want to live in the suburbs too. 6. My sister will also be back before noon.-My sister will be back before noon too. 7. He also comes to work by bus.-He comes to school by bus too. 8. Rachel is also a friendly person.-Rachel is a studious person too.

Page 71 A. 2. We didn't see any good 3. He didn't make any mistakes 4. They don't have any pretty 5. The teacher didn't teach us any important 6. We didn't learn any new 7. There aren't any flowers 8. There aren't any rich 9. We don't have any good

  B. 2. Pour me some coffee. 3. We need some more chairs in this room. 4. There are some boys in the hall. 5. She wants some oranges. 6. They told us about some of their experiences. 7. There are some good seats left for the play tonight. 8. You'll need some winter clothes in San Diego. 9. I see some $2 bills these days.

Page 72 2. some 3. any 4. any 5. some 6. any 7. any 8. any 9. some, any 10. any, some 11. some 12. any 13. any 14. some 15. some, any 16. any 17. any, any 18. any 19. some 20. any 21. any 22. some, any 23. any 24. some

Page 73   A. 2. There isn't someone at the door. 3. You didn't leave something on the hall table. 4. Bob won't bring someone with him. 5. I didn't lose the book somewhere downtown. 6. There isn't somebody in the next room. 7. Bobbie didn't go somewhere last night with her boss. 8. He doesn't have something important to say to you.

B. 2. There is something the matter witrh Toby's ear. 3. There was someone at the door. 4. We have spoken to somebody about it. 5. There does seem to be somebody in the office. 6. My keys are somewhere in this room. 7. I think there is something wrong with the calculator. 8. They could find her somewh189ere.

Page 74   2. ours 3. hers 4. yours 5. his 6. his 7. yours, mine 8. hers, mine 9. yours 10. yours 11. hers 12. theirs, ours 13. yours, mine 14. mine 15. mine 16. ours 17. mine 18. yours

Page 75   3. is hers 4. is mine 5. is Adrian's 6. is Miss Jefferson's 7. are theirs 8. are ours 9. are theirs 10. isn't mine 11. is his 12. is Mrs. Jones' 13. is Robert's 4. are ours, are theirs 15. is mine, is yours 16. must be his 17. is the teacher's 18. are theirs 19. is our landlord's 20. isn't mine, is my father's 21. is mine, is Virginia's 22. is Jim's little brother's

Page 76   2. my, hers 3. their, ours 4. our, theirs 5. my, his 6. their, ours 7. my, yours 8. his, hers 8. his, yours 10. their, ours 11. my, hers 12. my, hers 13. our, theirs 14. his, mine 15. his her, his her 16. my, hers 17. our, theirs 18. your, mine 19. their, ours 20. our, theirs

Page 77   2. ourselves 3. himself 4. themselves 5. ourselves 6. themselves 7. her-self 8. yourself yourselves 9. yourself yourselves 10. myself 11. myself 12. herself 13. himself 14. herself 15. itself himself, herself 16. itself 17. ourselves 18. yourself (yourselves)

Page 78   2. myself 3. herself 4. himself 5. ourselves 6. herself (himself) 7. herself 8. myself 9. themselves 10. himself (herself) 11. themselves 12. himself (herself) 13. myself 14. yourself 15. themselves 16. himself 17. themselves 18. yourself (yourselves) 19. herself 20. myself

Page 79   2. by themselves 3. by myself 4. by herself (by himself) 5. by himself 6. by himself 7. by himself 8. by herself 9. by yourself (yourselves) 10. by myself 11. by themselves, by themselves 12. by oneself 13. by herself 14. by myself 15. by himself 16. by itself 17. by himself 18. by itself 19. by ourselves 20. by yourself (yourselves)

Page 80   2. have finished 3. has visited 4. has returned 5. have lost 6. have been 7. has rained 8. have learned 9. have told 10. have heard 11. have lent 12. has gone 13. have made 14. has seen 15. has made, lost

Page 81   2. went 3. have read 4. read 5. have been 6. has had 7. fell 8. saw 9. jumped, ran 10. have tried 11. went 12. have completed 13. started 14. had 15. have given 16. have, been 17. was 18. have learned 19. began, ended 20. has lost (lost)

Page 82   2. lived 3. worked 4. has worked 5. studied 6. have studied 7. has spoken 8. worked 9. has worked 10. left, has worked 11. has studied 12. have studied 13. has been 14. felt 15. bought, have driven 16. have, been

Page 83   2. They have been talking 3. I have been traveling 4. He has been sleeping 5. It has been raining 6. He has been studying 7. We have been using 8. She has been teaching 9. They have been living 10. The two nations have been quarreling 11. She has been taking 12. They have been looking 13. He has been doing 14. Lynn has been working 15. You have been arguing

Page 84   A-B. 2. She has not been teaching, She hasn't been teaching-Has she been teaching 3. It has not been snowing, It hasn't been snowing-Has it been snowing 4. I have not spoken to, I haven't spoken to-Have I spoken to 5. You have not been studying, You haven't been studying-Have you been studying 6. He has not been, He hasn't been-Has he been 7. She has not been taking, She hasn't been taking-Has she been taking 8. We have not been discussing, We haven't been discussing-Have we been discussing 9. She has not been, She hasn't been-Has she been 10. They have not returned, They haven't returned-Have they returned11. He has not known, He hasn't known-Has he known 12. Joel has not found, Joel hasn't found-Has Joel found 13. You have not been, You haven't been-Have you been 14. He has not told, He hasn't told-Has he told 15. Mr. Garvin has not left, Mr. Garvin hasn't left-Has Mr. Garvin left 16. They have not been having, They haven't been having-Have they been having 17. He has not been feeling, He hasn't been feeling-Has he been feeling 18. They have not been married, They haven't been married-Have they been married

Page 85   2. How long have they been 3. How long have they been 4. How long has he been 5. How long has she been 6. How long have they been 7. How long have they been 8. How long has he been 9. How long has it been 10. How long has she been 11. How long has he been 12. How long have they occupied 13. How long has he been 14. How long has she been 15. How long have they been 16. How long has the dog been 17. How long has he been 18. How long has she been

Page 86   A. 2. since 1981 (?) 3. since June (?) 4. since Wednesday (?) 5. since Tuesday (?) 6. since last year (?) 7. since seven o'clock (?) 8. since Tuesday (?) 9. since one o'clock (?) 10. since June (?)

B. 2. for two months (?) 3. for four years (?) 4. for many years (?) 5. for twelve hours (?) 6. for many years (?) 7. for four years (?) 8. for a week (?) 9. for three days (?) 10. for six months (?)

Page 87   A. 2. already 3. yet (already), yet 4. already 5. already 6. already 7. yet 8. yet (already) 9. yet (already), yet 10. yet (already) 11. yet 12. already

B-C. 2. No, the mail hasn't arrived yet.-Yes, the mail has already arrived. 3. No, I haven't finished my homework yet.-Yes, I have already finished my homework. 4. No, Mr. Dole hasn't returned from lunch yet.- Yes, Mr. Dole has already returned from lunch. 5. No, I haven't paid that bill yet.-Yes, I have already paid that bill. 6. No the meeting hasn't begun yet.-Yes, the meeting has already begun. 7. No, George hasn't found a job yet.-Yes, George has already found a job. 8. No, the boat hasn't sailed yet.-Yes, the boat has already sailed. 9. No, I haven't bought the tickets for the game yet.-Yes, I have already bought the tickets for the game. 10. No, I haven't ridden in Pam's new car yet.-Yes, I have already ridden in Pam's new car.

Page 88   2. told 3. told 4. told, said 5. tell, said 6. said 7. told 8. told, tell 9. told 10. tell

Page 89   11. told, said 12. said 13. Tell, said, said 14. tells, tell 15. said 16. told 17. told 18. tell 19. said 20. told 21. said 22. told 23. told 24. told 25. tell 26. told

Page 90   B. 2. Gene told me that 3. She told me that 4. Joseph told me that 5. George told me that 6. I told him that 7. The student told me that 8. The man told me that 9. The farmer told me that 10. The man told me that 11. He also told me that 12. Jean told me that

C. 2. She said that 3. I said that 4. We said that 5. The manager said that 6. The doctor said that 7. He said that 8. I said that 9. We said that 10. I said that 11. He said that 12. I said that

Page 91   A. 3. Len may be 4. Loretta may lend 5. She may call 6. Frank may offer 7. The weather may get 8. She may be 9. You may feel 10. It may not rain 11. We may be 12. He may not want 13. They may go 14. They may go

B. 2. He may pass all his examinations. I'm not sure. 3. He may be back 4. She may drive 5. We may be going 6. We may be going 7. She may wait 8. We may see 9. She may lend 10. They may take

Page 92   2. had left 3. had captured 4. had gone 5. had taken 6. had made 7. had met 8. had left 9. had happened 10. had been 11. had given 12. had prepared 13. had done 14. had had 15. had seen

Page 93   2. as large as 3. as wide as 4. so intelligent as 5. as early as 6. as beautifully as 7. as quickly as 8. as fast as 9. as well as 10. as carefully as 11. as regularly as 12. as early as 13. as easily as 14. as hard as 15. as soon as 16. so cold today as 17. as good as 18. as often as

Page 94   2. She said she could not do 3. She said her name was Smith. 4. I thought I could finish 5. predicted that it would rain 6. Mr. Wick said he was very 7. complained that she had a 8. He thought he might finish 9. I did not think I could complete 10. promised that the error would not occur 11. He said the mail would certainly be 12. students thought they were making 13. They said the weather would probably be 14. I thought it would rain 15. He hoped he could get 16. I didn't think I would see 17. She said she might be 18. I thought he was out

Page 95   A. 19. Did he say she couldn't do 20. He complained that nobody believed a word he said. 21. I was certain... would go 22. She told me that prices were sure 23. promised faithfully that he would deliver 24. He hoped he might reach 25. He said that he had known 26. She said she had lived 27. She thought she could get 28. He said he was taking 29. declared that the prisoner wasn't guilty 30. They felt sure the battle would be 31. I wondered what... chairman would introduce. 32. He swore he had never seen

B. 2. They think they have found... they are mistaken. 3. He thinks the mail will surely be 4. The paper says it will rain 5. She says her name is 6. He says that he is too 7. I do not think he can finish 8. He says he'll be 9. I do not think she'll come. 10. Does he say he'll call 11. She promises she'll try to do 12. He tells me he thinks prices are going 13. He says he has found 14. She says she can't understand what I mean.

Page 96   2. They have to stay there 3. You have to send it 4. He has to have more practice 5. They have to help her 6. You have to speak 7. He has to spend 8. You have to write 9. We have to leave 10. We have to learn 11. You have to insure 12. I have to take 13. Roger has to give 14. They have to spend 15. You have to pay 16. You have to help

Page 97   A-B. Students use their own words to complete the sentences in Exercise B. 2. She had to have-She will have to have 3. Boris had to have-Boris will have to have 4. Everyone had to work-Everyone will have to work 5. He had to learn-He'll have to learn 6. I had to go-I'll have to go 7. She had to return-She'll have to return 8. He had to see-He'll have to see 9. We had to lend-We'll have to lend 10. You had to spend-You'll have to spend 11. We had to stay-

We'll have to stay 12. They had to leave-They'll have to leave 13. You had to send-You'll have to send 14. He had to give-He'll have to give

Page 98   A-B. 2. They won't have to buy-Will they have to buy 3. I don't have to cash-Do I have to cash 4. He didn't have to pay-Did he have to pay 5. They didn't have to go-Did they have to go 6. She doesn't have to take-Does she have to take 7. He doesn't have to write-Does he have to write 8. We won't have to take -shall we have to take 9. They didn't have to wait-Did they have to wait 10. They don't have to learn-Do they have to learn 11. I don't have to go-Do I have to go 12. We didn't have to wait-Did we have to wait 13. He doesn't have to get up-Does he have to get up 14. They didn't have to telephone-Did they have to telephone 15. I won't have to lend-Shall I have to lend 16. She doesn't have to help-Does she have to help

Page 99   2. How long did they have to wait there? 3. Why did the children have to stay indoors? 4. Why did they have to leave the party early? 5. When does he have to go to Denver? 6. How long will he have to stay there? 7. How much did they have to pay for their medicine? 8. When do I have to go to the dentist again? 9. What time will you have to come back? 10. Why does he have to go to the post office? 11. How many new words does each student have to learn every day? 12. How often does she have to go there? 13. How much did they have to leave as a deposit? 14. What time does he have to leave? 15. Where do you have to sign your name? 16. Why does Mary have to do all the housework? 17. Whom shall I have to ask for the money?

Page 100   2. on 3. into 4. out 5. into 6. from 7. of 8. into 9. on (in) 10. at... in 11. in... at 12. from 13. on 14. in 15. at... of 16. in... of 17. beside 18. at... in 19. out 20. over 21. at... of 22. under (off)... across (onto) 23. to 24. at... in 25. down (through)... in (at) 26. at 27. for... in... in 28. into... through

Page 101   2. by (at) 3. for 4. since 5. for 6. since 7. until (till, at) 8. for (none). 9. in... At 10. in... to 11. for 12. at... at 13. in 14. at (by)... of 15. by 16. from... to 17. in... to 18. to 19. during 20. at 21. in 22. in 23. at... at 24. since 25. at 26. in 27. for

Page 102   2. with 3. in 4. at 5. on... in 6. with 7. of 8. for 9. in 10. over 11. for 12. by... by 13. with 14. in 15. By 16. by 17. in... with 18. into 19. on 20. of 21. for 22. to... of 23. to 24. for... with... to 25. between 26. from 27. in... with 28. At... in... of... for... in

Page 103   A. 2. That house was destroyed by fire. 3. The concert was enjoyed very much by the audience. 4. That book was taken from the desk by Bob. 5. The cake will be eaten by Walter. 6. The report has been finished by Beth. 7. The tickets will be left at the box office by Ms. Duke. 8. A box of flowers has just been left for you by the messenger. 9. The thief was easily captured by the police. 10. The lecture was attended by many people. 11. We were very much disappointed by the movie. 12. The export division is managed by Mr. Jones. 13. The money was returned by John last night.

B. 2. The fire destroyed the entire city. 3. The enemy captured the town. 4. Someone has stolen the money from my purse. 5. Mary found the book. 6. John has returned the book. 7. Many people all over the world read the book. 8. Paula delivers the mail.

Page 104   2. A dancing class was started by them last week. 3. The accident was seen by Mr. Smith. 4. The report was left on the desk by him. 5. This film will soon be seen by everybody. 6. The report has just been finished by him. 7. The war was followed by an economic crisis.

8. My briefcase has been taken by somebody. 9. Our written work was returned to us by the teacher. 10. Books are bought from that store by Valerie. 11. By noon the report had been finished by her. 12. The little boy was bitten by the mad dog. 13. The fog is blown away by the wind by midmorning. 14. You will be chosen by the committee as its representative. 15. The plate and the glass were broken by the maid. 16. The street was lined by tall telegraph poles. 17. The event was immediately reported by the newspapers. 18. The sound of music was heard by us. 19. Five suspects have been arrested by the police. 20. Our dog was played with by the neighborhood children. 21. He was ordered to take a long rest by the doctor. 22. The house was struck by lightning.

Page 105 2. It should be sent to us at once by them. 3. The mail is being delivered now by the mailman. 4. It has to be finished by him today. 5. He is being held for further questioning by the police. 6. A new group may be organized by them next week. 7. The package ought to be sent by you by registered mail. 8. The city is being defended bravely by the citizens. 9. The meeting cannot be held by them in that room. 10. The merchandise may be delivered by them while we are out. 11. The bill has to be paid by him before the first of the month. 12. The bill may be paid for us by him. 13. That question is being debated by Congress today. 14. For the time being, that group is being taught by Karen. 15. The plant ought to be watered by you once a week. 16. The merchandise is being shipped by the company today. 17. They must be warned by us of the danger. 18. The house couldn't be sold by them at that price. 19. My aunt is being sent to Europe by them on a special mission. 20. The package should be insured by you.

Page 106 A-B. 2. This must not be finished, mustn't be finished-Must this be finished today? 3. The letter has not been sent yet, hasn't been sent yet-Has the letter been sent already (yet)? 4. The book was not published, wasn't published-Was the book published 5. The class is not taught, isn't taught-Is the class taught 6. The merchandise is not being sent, isn't being sent-Is the merchandise being sent 7. The thief has not been caught, hasn't been caught-Has the thief been caught 8. The fire was not started, wasn't started-Was the fire started 9. The chairs have not been put, haven't been put-Have the chairs been put 10. The jewels were not stolen, weren't stolen-Were the jewels stolen 11. The book will not be published, won't be published-Will the book be published 12. The lecture was not attended, wasn't attended-Was the lecture attended 13. The first prize was not won, wasn't won-Was the first prize won 14. The accident was not caused, wasn't caused-Was the accident caused 15. Our exercises will not be corrected, won't be corrected-Will our exercises be corrected 16. The house was not completely destroyed, wasn't completely destroyed-Was the house completely destroyed 17. The tickets have not been purchased, haven't been purchased-Have the tickets been purchased 18. The bridge was not designed, wasn't designed-Was the bridge designed 19. The contract will not be signed, won't be signed-Will the contract be signed 20. The packages are not delivered, aren't delivered-Are the packages delivered 21. The cries of the child were not heard, weren't heard-Were the cries of the child heard 22. The house was not struck, wasn't struck-Was the house struck

Page 107 2. How was the building destroyed? 3. When will the merchandise be delivered? 4. By whom had the money been stolen? 5. Where was the child finally found? 6. In what kind of accident was he injured? 7. What time is the mail delivered? 8. When must the contract be signed by Mr. Smith? 9. Where will the tickets be left? 10. In what year was San Francisco nearly destroyed by earthquake? 11. Where was the book published? 12. What was he operated on for? 13. Why was the boy punished? 14. Where was the note left? 15. In what month was the city captured by the enemy? 16. Where was the money put? 17. When will the bridge be finished? 18. Who designed it?

Page 108 2. was supposed to sail 3. was supposed to come 4. is supposed to be 5. is supposed to bring 6. was supposed to be written 7. was supposed to mail 8. is supposed to leave 9. was supposed to take 10. supposed to meet 11. is supposed to meet, is supposed to meet 12. supposed to write 13. am supposed to be 14. is supposed to take 15. is supposed to be published

Page 109 2. I never used to make 3. The accounting department used to be 4. Tom used to be a good employee and used to work hard. 5. I used to buy 6. This building used to be occupied 7. Betty used to have charge 8. Gary used to play 9. Laura used to go 10. He never used to do 11. He used to take 12. All meetings used to be held 13. Marcus used to be 14. I used to smoke 15. Mr. Earl used to work 16. I never used to catch cold. 17. It used to be my custom to smoke (I used to smoke)

Page 110 2. They would rather walk-They'd rather walk 3. We would rather spend the summer at home than in-We'd rather spend the summer at home than in 4. The doctor says that he would rather examine-The doctor says that he'd rather examine 5. I would rather not mention-I'd rather not mention 6. I would rather eat at home than in-I'd rather eat at home than in 7. He would rather meet us-He'd rather meet us 8. I would rather speak-I'd rather speak 9. I would rather drive a small car than-I'd rather drive a small car than 10. Jean would rather study in this class than in 11. I would rather do-I'd rather do 12. He would rather live-He'd rather live 13. I would rather live-I'd rather live 14. I would rather work in my garden than play-I'd rather work in my garden than play 15. I would rather see a good movie than go-I'd rather see a good movie than go 16. He would rather attend, I would rather go-He'd rather attend, I'd rather go

Page 111 2. She had better rest, She'd better rest 3. Betty had better give 4. She had better not see, She'd better not see 5. They had better save, They'd better save 6. You had better not mention, You'd better not mention 7. You had better send, You'd better send 8. You had better not tell, You'd better not tell 9. You had better tell, You'd better tell 10. Neil had better prepare 11. You had better not drive, You'd better not drive 12. You had better not give, You'd better not give 13. You had better notify, You'd better notify 14. You had better spend, You'd better spend

Page 112 2. hasn't he? 3. isn't he? 4. doesn't she? 5. can't she? 6. didn't you? 7. isn't it? 8. wasn't it? 9. don't you? 10. don't they? 11. won't you? 12. haven't you? 13. aren't they? 14. doesn't it? 15. doesn't it? 16. aren't they? 17. didn't I? 18. wasn't she? 19. couldn't you?

Page 113 2. have you? 3. will you? 4. is it? 5. was it? 6. did they? 7. did she? 8. was he? 9. does she? 10. will he? 11. does it? 12. did you? 13. have I? 14. is she? 15. have you? 16. can he? 17. should I? 18. will we? 19. would they?

Page 114 2. isn't he? 3. has she? 4. isn't it? 5. don't you? 6. weren't you? 7. don't they? 8. do they? 9. doesn't it? 10. will we? 11. didn't you? 12. did you? 13. can't she? 14. does he? 15. isn't it? 16. doesn't it? 17. isn't she? 18. hasn't she? 19. isn't it? 20. isn't there? 21. didn't it? 22. didn't they? 23. won't you? 24. has it? 25. hasn't she?

Page 115 C-D-E. 2. doesn't she; wrote-didn't she; will write-won't she 3. isn't he; was-wasn't he; will be-won't he 4. doesn't he; made-didn't he; will make-won't he 5. doesn't she; spent-didn't she; will spend-won't she 6. doesn't he; came-didn't he; will come-won't he 7. isn't he; was-wasn't he; will be-won't he 8. aren't there; were-weren't there; will be-won't there 9. aren't they; were-weren't they; will be-won't they 10. don't they; watched-didn't they, will watch-won't they 11. don't you; enjoyed-didn't you; will enjoy-won't you 12. isn't it; was delivered-wasn't it; will be delivered-won't it 13. don't you; spent-didn't you; will spend-won't you 14. doesn't she; had to work-didn't she; will have to work-won't she 15. isn't he; was-wasn't he; will be-won't he 16. don't you; had-didn't you; will have-won't you 17. doesn't it; arrived-didn't it; will arrive-won't it 18. don't they; visited-didn't they; will visit-won't they 19. don't you; got-didn't you; will get-won't you 20. doesn't he; sat-didn't he; will sit-won't he 21. doesn't she; worked-didn't she; will work-won't she 22. isn't he; was-wasn't he; will be-won't he

Page 116 2. There is 3. There is 4. It is 5. It is 6. It is 7. There is 8. There is 9. It is 10. It is 11. It is 12. It is 13. There is 14. There is 15. It is 16. There is 17. It is

Page 117 2. There 3. It 4. It 5. There 6. It 7. It 8. There 9. It 10. It 11. There 12. It 13. It 14. There 15. It 16. It 17. There 18. It 19. There 20. It 21. There 22. It 23. It 24. There

Page 118 2. It is important to learn new words every day. 3. It is very rewarding to study with Ms. Nathan. 4. It is foolish to pay so much money for a car that is old. 5. It is dangerous to drive so fast. 6. It is interesting to travel in foreign countries. 7. It is often helpful to be able to speak a foreign language. 8. It is unfair to blame Rocky for that mistake. 9. For a lot of students, it is not interesting to study grammar. 10. It is important to understand grammar. 11. It is almost impossible for me to get up early in the morning. 12. It is faster to go by bus than by car. 13. It is not easy for a soprano to sing in such a low key. 14. It will be difficult to explain this matter to him. 15. It is foolish to work twelve hours a day at your age. 16. It will be pleasant to spend the afternoon at the beach. 17. It would be unwise to call her at this late hour. 18. It is not satisfying to eat quickly. l9. It is not easy to accept their apologies. 20. It is demanding to be comfortable in such hot weather. 21. It is their goal to compete for the top prize.

Page 119 2. There are a lot 3. There are two 4. There are several 5. There is a 6. There is a 7. There are a lot 8. There are two 9. There is a 10. There are two 11. There is only 12. There are two 13. There is a 14. There are several 15. There are a lot 16. There is a 17. There is an 18. There are curtains 19. There are a lot 20 There is a 21. There is a 22. There are two 23. There are some

Page 120 2. studying 3. going 4. waiting 5. buying 6. traveling 7. coming 8. listening 9. using 10. holding 11. receiving 12. painting 13. hitting 14. taking 15. going16. making

Page 121 2. of swimming 3. in spelling 4. calling 5. of seeing 6. of waiting 7. reading 8. living 9. of finding 10. in helping 11. attending 12. of moving 13. on helping 14. holding 15. about starting 16. of leaving 17. to seeing 18. of seeing

Page 122 To be completed by the students in their own words.

Page 123 A-B. 2. likes taking-likes to take 3. neglected telling-neglected to tell 4. prefer meeting-prefer to meet 5. start working-start to work 6. continue taking-continue to take 7. loves working-loves to work 8. intends leaving-intends to leave 9. hates leaving-hates to leave 10. start coming-start to come 11. likes studying-likes to study 12. prefers taking-prefers to take 13. begin increasing-begin to increase 14. continued building-continued to build 15. hates doing-hates to do

Page 124 2. will have seen 3. will have forgotten 4. will have died 5. will have been finished-will have been turned in 6. shall have finished 7. shall have been 8. will have forgotten 9. will have become 10. shall have learned 11. will not have learned 12. will have been signed 13. will have learned 14. will have taken

Page 125 [Other answers may be correct.] 2. is teaching, is substituting 3. was working 4. are going to take 5. came 6. was coming met, to sell 7. have been 8. is ringing 9. had seen 10. have read (read) 11. shall have completed 12. came, was leaving 13. was shining 14. begins, ends 15. go 16. is knocking 17. has been heard 18. has studied (has been studying) 19. studied 20. is coming (will come)

Page 126 2. caught 3. Is, crossing 4. Does, walk 5. had left 6. will have visited (will be visiting) 7. will have been 8. had written 9. studies, see, is studying 10. will be doing, call 11. were you doing 12. has Harry been 13. was, has been 14. are you going to go (are you going) 15. had shot 16. was shining, had disappeared 17. began, ended had met

Page 127 2. tell, flatter 3. had lost 4. were driving, had 5. jumped 6. had come, gone 7. tripped, entered (was entering) 8. was chosen 9. has been seen 10. had taken 11. see, drive 12. dancing, hasn't healed 13. to go 14. did you go 15. will you go (are you going to go, are you going) 16. do you usually go 17. are you doing

Page 128 2. Sam has always been 3. He often goes 4. He seldom stays 5. She cheerfully accepted 6. She plays the piano well. 7. at our home tonight. 8. She has never spoken 9. Alice carefully replaced 10. Al is always late 11. He has always prepared 12. in the park on Sunday.

Page 129 13. We usually go 14. Do you ever go 15. I never go 16. that matter on Tuesday. 17. an answer in the morning. 18. Have you ever visited 19. Do you usually eat 20. Have you ever eaten 21. your exercises yet? 22. I have often spoken 23. Have you ever spoken 24. Has he always been 25. I have never been 26. that book twice. 27. I have never read-Have you ever read 28. in college last week. 29. He is often too busy 30. for Denver tomorrow. 31. Does she sometimes forget 32. Does she generally get up 33. Has he always been 34. Nobody ever has 35. his work cheerfully. 36. He rarely does his exercises carefully. 37. for California tomorrow. 38. I met him there yesterday.

Page 130 2. He is now studying engineering at Columbia University. 3. He was so excited he could hardly think. 4. The light was so bright that we had to cover our eyes from time to time. 5. She said that he had already had three operations. 6. I didn't even know that it was you who was calling me. 7. Throw me a kiss from the bus. 8. In a new skirt, Karen went to see the mayor. 9. Louise sometimes comes to our house for the lesson, and I sometimes go to hers. 10. I used to like the theater a lot, but now I go to the movies every night. 11. Of course I always speak German with my family and friends. 12. He is now studying French as well as English. 13. He has been here two years; perhaps it is even more than that. 14. It was so cold that summer that we had to wear our overcoats now and then. 15. I have to write a lot of letters in English every day. 16. He said that he had already seen that movie. 17. He seldom comes to the lesson on time. 18. Simon gave me your message this morning. 19. Please read the whole sentence slowly. 20. We went to the theater last night.

Page 131 A. 2. still 3. still 4. still 5. anymore 6. anymore 7. anymore 8. anymore 9. still, anymore 10. still 11. still 12. anymore 13. still 14. still, anymore

B. 2. He isn't president of the club anymore. 3. They don't live on State Street anymore. 4. They don't visit each other regularly anymore. 5. He is not in love with her anymore. 6. They are not living in Quito anymore. 7. We don't see them at the club on Saturday night anymore. 8. It is not raining anymore.

Page 132 2. said the plane would probably get in 3. said he had to finish 4. said she'd get well 5. said everyone had to 6. said he had seen 7. said she had read 8. told her boyfriend she couldn't go 9. told me he'd finish 10. told him the lights weren't working 11. I told the waitress the bill was wrong. 12. said he was only 13. said he could meet 14. said she didn't do

Page 133 2. asked me where I was going. 3. asked whether (if) I was going to 4. asked whether (if) I had mailed . . . for her. 5. asked me where I was going on my 6. asked he whether (if) she liked 7. asked me how I was 8. asked the storekeeper what the price . . . was. 9. asked me when I would get back from my 10. asked her what time it was. 11. asked when we would land. 12. asked whether (if) it took longer 13. asked me what time it was. 14. asked me how long I had studied

Page 134 2. his name is 3. it is 4. she lives 5. my car cost 6. he put 7. we have 8. it is 9. he is 10. I was 11. she lives 12. she lived 13. she was 14. I had studied 15. he was 16. Helen is 17. I put 18. he lives 19. I would 20. I was 21. he could 22. I was

Page 135 2. He wants to know where Miss Dale went. 3. I wonder what time it is. 4. wants to know... letter is. 5. like to know how much this costs. 6. wants to know how he is 7. seems to know when he is 8. asked me when Mr. Saki would get 9. didn't know what the price... was. 10. know where he is? 11. asked whether he had finished 12. ask him whether he lives 13. forget where I put it. 14. asked him what it meant. 15. know where she is going 16. tell me what time he was coming 17. any idea where it is 18. don't know whether she took 19. know how well she speaks 20. sure whether he is coming 21. tell anyone where he was going 22. don't know whether he returned

Page 136 A. 2. told us not to make 3. told me to try 4. begged us please to send 5. asked us please to sit 6. told me not to forget 7. asked us please to be... when we wrote our 8. told me angrily not to make 9. said to come 10. told him not to call 11. begged me please not to mention 12. told the boy to put 13. told us to type our 14. told him never to try (told him not to ever try)

B. 2. The teacher told me to stay 3. The teacher told me not to make 4. The teacher told me to look... but not to open it. 5. The teacher told me to stop talking 6. The teacher told me to sit... in my seat. 7. The teacher told me to be quiet while she was talking. 8. The teacher told me to pay... what she said.

Page 137 1. said the students needed-said these exercises were difficult for her-said she

didn't feel-said nobody could do-said she would be-said she might be-said she had already seen
2. asked me where that girl lived-asked me how old I was-asked me what time it was-asked me where I was going-asked me how long I had studied-asked me whether I liked 3. don't know where she lives-don't know what time it is-don't know where they went-don't know whether she speaks-don't know how long she has been studying-don't know what her first name is
4. told them to wait-told them to come-told them not to mention-told them to do-told them not to go

Page 138 A-B. 2. They shouldn't make-They ought not to make 3. I should spend-I ought to spend 4. He shouldn't eat-He ought not to eat 5. You should learn -You ought to learn 6. You should ask-You ought to ask 7. He should get-He ought to get 8. You really should go-You really ought to go 9. Someone should tell -Someone ought to tell 10. No one should spend-No one ought to spend 11. She shouldn't waste-She ought not to waste 12. I should write-I ought to write 13. You shouldn't work-You ought not to work 14. You should rest-You ought to rest 15. We should pay-We ought to pay

Page 139 2. You should have gone 3. She ought to have prepared 4. You should have typed 5. You ought not to have said 6. We ought to have called 7. You should have visited 8. She ought to have been put 9. The letter should have been sent 10. You should have spoken 11. They ought to have bought 12. He should have told 13. You should have paid 14. We should have gone 15. You ought to have put 16. You shouldn't have been

Page 140 Students answer in their own words.

Page 141 A. 2. I'll go 3. I'll give 4. he'll get 5. we'll be 6. he'll find 7. he'll have 8. we'll go 9. I'll talk 10. I'll go

B. 1. find 2. is. 3. turn 4. save 5. drive 6. calls 7. learn

Page 142 A. 2. he would make-he'd make 3. we would take-we'd take 4. he would not feel-he wouldn't feel 5. he would have-he'd have 6. people would respect 7. I would read-I'd read 8. he would get-he'd get

B. 1. If I owned 2. If she worked 3. If I knew how 4. If Louis knew 5. If he did not waste

Page 143 A. 2. If today were 3. If I were 4. If today were 5. If the weather were 6. If Pete were 7. If you were

B. 1. I would feel 2. they would not be able to live 3. I would go 4. she would know 5. I would tell 6. I would live 7. he would try

Page 144 A. 2. he would have been 3. I would have come 4. we would have gone 5. you would not have caught 6. I would have written 7. I would have gone 8. I would have helped

B. 1. If I had known 2. If the weather had been 3. if I had known 4. if I had worn 5. If he had studied

Page 145 A-B. 2. If she studied, she would pass; If she had studied, she would have passed 3. If I had, I would buy; If I had had, I would have bought 4. If I saw, I would give; If I had seen, I would have given 5. If you turned, we would be; If you had turned, we would have been 6. If she saved, she would be able to go; If she had saved, she would have been able to go 7. If the weather were, we would go; If the weather had been, we would have gone 8. If he had, he would go; If he had had, he would have gone 9. If they worked, they would learn; If they had worked they would have learned 10. If you went, you would have; If you had gone, you would have had 11. If Eva were, the party would be; If Eva had been, the party would have been 12. If we hurried, we could get; If we had hurried, we could have gotten 13. If Phil worked, he might get; If Phil had worked, he might have gotten 14. If I didn't have to study, I would go; If I hadn't had to study, I would have gone 15. If they invited, I would go; If they had invited, I would have gone 16. If it rained, we wouldn't go; If it had rained, we wouldn't have gone 17. If they lent, I would be able to go; If they had lent, I would have been able to go 18. If I felt, I would go; If I had felt, I would have gone 19. If I were not, I would be glad; If I had not been, I would have been glad

Page 146 C., D. Students answer in their own words.

Page 147 E. Students answer in their own words.

Page 148 F. Students answer in their own words.

G. 2. I would not have said 3. I had known 4. I would have been 5. I will stay 6. I want 7. I would like to 8. weather is

Page 149 9. I would not have ignored 10. it would have been 11. I would not have caught 12. they had known 13. I would not work... I would be 14. I shall play 15. we would have caught 16. I had known

H. Students answer in their own words.

Page 150 1. rains 2. is 3. go 4. get 5. get 6. invite 7. rises 8. call 9. rains 10. gets 11. arrives 12. do not arrive 13. see 14. sit 15. see

Page 151 B. 2. I wish you would mail this letter right away, Kevin. 3. I wish you would be creative in your writing. 4. I wish you wouldn't make any mistakes. 5. I wish you would help me with this problem.

Page 152 A-B. 2. Liz left right after lunch, and Bob did, too-Liz left right after lunch, and so did Bob. 3. and I am too-so am I 4. and I shall, too-so will I 5. yours is, too-so is yours 6. I did, too-so did I 7. her brother is, too-so is her brother 8. his wife has, too-so has his wife 9. his assistant was, too-so was his assistant 10. I did, too-so did I 11. I did, too-so did I 12. her sister will, too-so will her sister 13. they do, too-so do they 14. she can, too-so can she 15. Cy has, too-so has Cy

Page 153 A-B. 2. I didn't either-neither did I 3. her sister won't either-neither will her sister 4. I haven't either-neither have I 5. I hadn't either-neither had I 6. I wouldn't either-neither would I 7. I can't either-neither can I 8. I don't either-neither do I 9. mine isn't either-neither is mine 10. my wife doesn't either-neither does she 11. Mr. Barker wasn't either-neither was Mr. Barker 12. my friend couldn't either-neither could my friend 13. your son won't either-neither will your son 14. they don't either-neither do they

Page 154 2. doesn't 3. can't 4. won't 5. did 6. don't 7. is 8. do 9. will 10. has 11. haven't 12. doesn't 13. doesn't 14. isn't 15. don't 16. I'm not 17. do 18. don't 19. don't 20. I am not

Page 155 2. won't 3. will 4. does 5. is 6. are 7. has 8. did 9. isn't 10. can 11. can't 12. does 13. would 14. can 15. will 16. do 17. have 18. can 19. can't 20. don't 21. are 22. do

Page 156 A-B. 2. Isn't Conrad changing-Why isn't Conrad changing 3. Won't Helene be-Why won't Helene be 4. Won't she be-Why won't she be 5. Didn't Andrea take-Why didn't Andrea take 6. Doesn't Colleen like-Why doesn't Colleen like 7. Don't we like-Why don't we like 8. Aren't they going-Why aren't they going 9. Didn't Mr. Donahue bring-Why didn't Mr. Donahue bring 10. Isn't it-Why isn't it 11. Wasn't it-Why wasn't it 12. Hasn't it-Why hasn't it-13. Aren't the Starskys moving-Why aren't the Starskys moving

Page 157 2. Which month comes 3. What is 4. Who drove 5. What caused 6. Which umbrella belongs 7. Which notebook is 8. Which bus goes 9. Who lives 10. Which country is 11. Who is 12. What causes 13. Who has 14. What ocean is 15. Who won 16. Which book is 17. Who is 18. Who is doing

Page 158 A. 2. She must have taken 3. They must have gone 4. Roy must have studied 5. She must have studied 6. You must have seen 7. The bank must have been robbed 8. He must have come

B. 2. They may have called 3. I may have left... I may have lost 4. They may have been 5. may have been stolen 6. The storm may have delayed

Page 159 C. Students answer using their own words.

D. 2. Prof. Wiley may have learned Spanish in South America--I'm not sure. 3. Helen may have called while I was out--I'm not sure. 4. Mr. Reese may have been born in this country or Europe--I'm not sure. 5. Mary and Helen may have had an argument--I'm not sure. 6. He may have passed all his exams--I'm not sure. 7. Grace may have gone shopping this afternoon--I'm not sure. 8. They may have been married in Seattle--I'm not sure. 9. It may have rained during the night--I'm not sure. 10. The New York Yankees may have won the World Series last year--I'm not sure.

Page 160 A. 2. We'll have the oil changed, We'll get the oil changed 3. I should have the kitchen floor cleaned and waxed, I should get the kitchen floor cleaned and waxed. 4. You had those letters typed, You got those letters typed 5. They had the oxygen level checked, They got the oxygen level checked 6. Phil is going to have his winter coat dry-cleaned, He is going to get his winter coat dry-cleaned. 7. Did she have her computer repaired?, Did she get her computer repaired? 8. I should have the hole repaired, I should get the hole repaired.

Page 161 2. What a beautiful day! 3. What a good-looking boy! 4. How well Gail plays golf! 5. How fluently they speak English! 6. How tall Pauline is! 7. How hot it is today! 8. What a hot day! 9. What good taste you have in clothes! 10. What a gorgeous car! 11. What a lucky card player! 12. What beautiful weather! 13. How old Penny looks! 14. What an interesting movie! 15. How wide the lake is! 16. How strange that behavior was!

Page 162 2. I did write 3. Ed did take 4. But we did study 5. I do want 6. I did do 7. Do call 8. she does live 9. he did call 10. he did reach 11. they did show 12. he does attend 13. I did have 14. Do bring 15. Do visit 16. does seem

Page 163 2. of (about) 3. in 4. to (with) 5. for 6. to 7. for 8. in (at) 9. in (at) 10. by 11. to 12. to 13. at 14. at (to) 15. in 16. from 17. at (about)

Page 164 A-B. 2. The man whom you were speaking to is Dr. Evans.-The man you were speaking to is Dr. Evans. 3. This is the room which they found the clue in.-This is the room they found the clue in. 4. He is the kind of salesman whom it is difficult to get away from.-He is the kind of salesman it is difficult to get away from. 5. The person whom you should speak to is Miss Williams.-The person you should speak to is Miss Williams. 6. It is a subject which we shall never agree on.-It is a subject we shall never agree on. 7. The thing which they were arguing about was really of little importance. -The thing they were arguing about was really of little importance. 8. It is a place which you feel at home in.-It is a place you feel at home in. 9. It was Bob whom we had to wait for so long.-It was Bob we had to wait for so long. 10. It was Liz whom he borrowed the money from.-It was Liz he borrowed the money from. 11. The room which we study in is on the second floor. -The room we study in is on the second floor. 12. This is the street which they live on.-This is the street they live on. 13. I finally found the book which I was looking for.-I finally found the book I was looking for. 14. The students whom she studies with are mainly from South America.-The students she studies with are mainly from South America. 15. The fellow whom I roomed with was from Chicago.-The fellow I roomed with was from Chicago.

Page 165 2. Roberta, the mechanic, repaired 3. cannot, of course, reveal 4. Reese, the president of our class, spent 5. not, in the first place, tell 6. Scranton, Pennsylvania, on March 23, 1953, and 7. cannot, after all, live 8. way, do 9. Marlene, Henry's cousin, is.... Madison, Wisconsin. 10. you, Mr. Jones, on.... February 12, 1981? 11. Building, a famous landmark of the town,... fact, it... February 12, Lincoln's 12. tennis, swimming, and 13. Yesterday I met, quite by accident, three former schoolmates, Martinez, Palmer, and Stewart. 14. day, June 20, 1978.

Page 166 2. (no commas) 3. (no commas) 4. Mary, hair, 5. hands, tar, 6. (no commas) 7. (no commas) 8. Pace, story, 9. Wednesday, town, 10. Hemmingway, business, Glen Acres, 11. (no commas) 12. hair, morning, 13. (no commas) 14. (no commas) 15. Bridge, River,

Page 167 2. (no punctuation needed) 3. mechanic, 4. (no punctuation needed) 5. long time, 6. long time; 7. ambassadors, 8. go, 9. results, 10. cautious, 11. piano, 12. saxophone; 13. filthy, 14. time, 15. winter;

Page 168 2. room, around, other, then, enough, 3. Williams' store, groceries, repainted; consequence, 4. "I am sure, Mary," said William, "that you... house architect, Mr. W. James." 5. "Of course, Father, it's a pity," said Ellen, "that people don't... have done here." 6. Harrisburg, PA., to Albany, 7. (no punctuation needed) 8. We, Ida, Ethel, and I,... going; 9. Ben Reese's brother, Tim Reese, 10. Saturday, Jan. 16 1958,... we had had; however, day, Sunday, to me; but, of course, 11. climbed into the wagon; out, country. It was lovely. 12. eleven, meeting, 13. "I believe,"... visitor, "that Mr. Davis... once; yet, realize, naturally,... not a pleasant one." 14. Dr. Reynolds, 15. Commas, I noted, 16. Come here at once! I need you immediately! 17. Did you see her yesterday? Are you going to see her tomorrow? 18. When will we finish this exercise, Robert?

Page 169 No Exercises

Page 170 2. make 3. advise 4. into 5. beats 6. spilled 7. stole 8. until 9. advice 10. poured 11. rob 12. in 13. make 14. does 15. win 16. advise, pour, spilling 17. stole, in 18. as far as 19. farther, further

Page 171 No Exercises

Page 172 2. am used to 3. too 4. very 5. less 6. besides 7. beside 8. left 9. no 10. not 11. not, not 12. forgets 13. little, a few 14. used 15. few 16. are used to 17. few 18. too

Page 173 No Exercises

Page 174 2. borrow, lend 3. speak 4. talk 5. taught 6. despite the fact 7. have I seen 8. teach 9. learned 10. take 11. did the speaker mention 12. wait 13. could you find 14. foot- 15. In spite of the fact 16. make 17. speak 18. borrowing 19. further